OUT OF ORDER

CLINICAL WORK & UNCONSCIOUS PROCESS

MARTIN STANTON

REBUS PRESS

Rebus Press
76 Haverstock Hill
LONDON
NW3 2BE

ISBN 1 900877 10 4

FOR MY FATHER

ACKNOWLEDGEMENTS

This book is based on a series of lectures I presented at the French Institute in London in November/December 1994, and I should like to thank Michel Oriano, Charles Giry-Deloison and René Lacombe for their help in organizing this. I should also like to thank the audience, especially Val Parks, whose views and feedback have had an important effect on the form and content of this book.

In the development of my clinical work - reflected for better or worse in this book - I owe an inestimable debt to my patients, who hopefully fail to recognize themselves here; to Jacques Lacan, Serge Leclaire, and Maud Mannoni; and to Jean Laplanche, for all his help and support.

I should also like to thank the following: Mike Adams, Parveen Adams, Tessa Adams, Vicky Armstrong, Stephen Bann, Vivien Bar, Bernard Burgoyne, Aisling Campbell, Elizabeth Cowie, Chantal Dubertret, Rosemary Dunn, Cormac Gallagher, Gerald and Julia Gargiulo, Alison Hall, Kirsty Hall, Christopher Hauke, Meira Likierman, David Mayers, Oliver Rathbone, David Reason, Caspar Sinnige, Aidan Shingler, Harry and Terry Stanton. I am particularly indebted to Andrew Samuels for his constant and inspired criticism.

Above all, I should like to thank Kate and Liam for their love, sustenance, and for teaching me better ways.

Greenwich, London, September 1996

CONTENTS

CHAPTER 1

INTRODUCTION

What are you looking for when you start analysis? The 'cure' of a diagnosed condition, such as a phobia or depression? Or the removal of a distressing symptom, such as anxiety, shyness or the inability to express emotion? Or are you looking for more general benefits like 'enlightenment', psychic streetwiseness, or some encouragement to bite the bullet-truths of life?

Two distinct and sometimes conflicting impulses inform these questions: one is surgical, and aspires to identify and remove pathogenic material; and the other is educational, and aims to 'suggest out' (following Ferenczi's expression) misperceptions. For better or worse, since its inception a century ago, psychoanalysis has attempted to assimilate both these impulses into its everyday life. It has maintained a clinical presence, and elaborated a therapeutic practice with both neurotic and psychotic disorders; and it has also refined its interpretative methods to uncover unconscious processes and render them accessible, thereby enabling fresh and innovative forms of social and cultural criticism.

Despite this integration in clinical, educational, social, and cultural worlds, psychoanalysis still appears 'out of order'; 'out of order' in the mechanical sense that its various levels of critical and clinical operation are visibly no longer synchronized; 'out of order' also in so far as the unconscious is located outside the symbolic order, and failure of symbolization is more central to psychoanalytic enquiry than symbolic fullness and cohesion; and finally, 'out of order' in the current colloquial sense of infringement of others' desires and expectations.

Anyone who works as a psychoanalytic psychotherapist, or who teaches psychoanalytic studies in educational institutions, is familiar with the doubts, skepticism, and general hostility that surround the field. People enter the consulting room with serious questions about how - if at all - the psychoanalytic process works, and often bring profound skepticism with them after trying every alternative 'solution', including the psychopharmacological one. Negative impressions are further heightened by the daily press, which is both fascinated by the 'normalization' of psychoanalysis and the increased demand for it, particularly from eminent public figures; and profoundly distrustful of the power and omniscience assumed by some psychoanalysts, who sexually, financially or intellectually abuse their patients. In such cases, the press has proven ready to portray the abuse as a symptom of psychoanalysis, and not simply a specific case of malpractice. The standard headline here is usually a variant of: how can all these psychoanalysts have the cheek to claim to know how to live your life better than you ? The answer usually provided is: they can do it because they wish to extort large sums of money from you.

Such headlines may be hard to appreciate on any level, especially for those analysts who work with very difficult patients on a low or minimal fee basis, far away from press interest or concern. Nonetheless, the strong underlying anxieties, distrust, and disrespect expressed, do demand further analysis, in particular to enable critical differentiation between the workable and unworkable desires placed on psychoanalysis.

*

What, in the end, can psychoanalysis do for anyone? In recent years, psychoanalysts have not proven particularly willing to answer such an 'out of order' question, even though it is an everyday feature of their professional life. Trainee analysts are also not usually provided with any indication of how they might approach such a question - other than to dismiss it, and trust that it will become obvious as the analysis progresses. Potential patients equally have nowhere to turn for an answer, except to take at face value the basic guidelines concerning clinical methods, objectives, and ethics, which are provided by national registration bodies (BCP, 1997; UKCP, 1997).

This lack of concern for the out-of-orderness of psycho-analysis is relatively new. It certainly was not present during the late 1940s and early 1950s - the last period of rapid expansion in demand for psychoanalysis and psychoanalytic psychotherapy. At this time, two books in particular focussed specifically on public anxieties and the impossible demands placed on psychoanalysis: Samuel Lowy's *Should You Be Psychoanalyzed?* (Lowy,1963), and Karen Horney's *Are You Considering Psychoanalysis?* (Horney,1946). With their question-mark title, both these books playfully aimed to parody a popular trend of skepticism about psychoanalysis.

Lowy recounted an in-flight conversation with a fellow passenger who first asked rather intrusively what Lowy's employment was, and then proceeded to berate the psychoanalytic profession in general (Lowy,1963, pp.7-12). The passenger's main point was that analysis is an 'unnecessary treatment...given to people who have too much time on their hands and do not have to work for their livelihood' (p.9). Lowy painstakingly attempted to shift discussion towards 'clear productive areas' of psychoanalytic work, notably with somatoform disorders, and with the 'improvement of the patient's sense of responsibility and capacity for tolerance and friendship', but his interlocutor would have none of it. Finally and wittily, Lowy hit upon the winning argument: '"Would you equally object if the same people chose, instead of analysis, to spend the equivalent time in theatres, concert halls, social clubs, on tennis courts, and in bowling alleys; and if they did so without any pretense or chance of intellectual gain or spiritual uplift? " "No, actually I should not feel any disapproval...', the interlocutor admitted (p.10).

The important point to note about Lowy's critical strategy is that it centred around undermining the perception of psychoanalysis as an esoteric exercise, reserved for an elite which could privately fund itself. He replaced this perception with the notion of informed choice. According to him, anyone who so wished should be enabled to begin analysis on their own terms - with a basic (if minimal) engagement with both the curative and educational perspectives of psychoanalysis.

Karen Horney adopted a very similar approach, despite her different theoretical perspective: 'In the first place', she wrote, 'the patient wants to know whether he can be analyzed with some chances of success. Can analysis really do something about his drinking, his depressions? Or does he really need analysis? He may feel that if it were not for his eating spells or his fear of heights, he would be quite all right. Is this difficulty important enough to warrant a lengthy and incisive therapy?....Will analysis make him introspective and selfish? Does it stand for moral license? Does it interfere with artistic faculties? Will it disturb his marriage or religion? Will it so upset him that he cannot carry on with his job? Will it make him dependent on the analyst?' (Horney, 1946, pp.10-11).

In contrast, her answer to these questions was not to relate them to issues of social privilege, but to return them directly to the patient, and regard them as symptomatic of his or her neurotic distortion: 'In many instances, without knowing it, the patient needs more than factual information...his questions, his worries, his concerns may be greatly determined by his personal neurotic problem, by his specific fears, expectations, demands on himself, claims for specific prerogatives, by his pessimistic view of himself and of life in general' (p.11).

In their strategic apologies, both Lowy and Horney framed clinical work in psychoanalysis around a fundamental paradox: analysis was equally a unique address to the ills of Western culture, and deeply symptomatic of such ills. Lowy and Horney also portray psychoanalysis as a lone provider of help and support in processing misery, pain and suffering: it is 'one of the most valuable helps to our growth as human beings' (Horney, 1946, p. 13); but both also stress the residual toxicity of symptoms which psychoanalysis cannot hope to cure. In this context, both protest that analysts themselves require urgent protection from the toxicity of psychoanalysis (including its exaggerated claims to enlightenment, cure, and order), even though both recognize that protection from residual unconscious process is in effect impossible.

The strength of the Lowy-Horney popular approach - and its potential use-value for contemporary clinical training - derives from attention to the symptomatic aspects of clinical work itself: meticulous attention to all the twists and distortions provoked by the need, wish or desire to capture all that may elude interpretation. Psychoanalysis is 'out of order' precisely because it works primarily with all that resists interpretative order - failures, repressions, denials, and foreclosures of any supposed human natural order. To propose a residual and unprocessable unconscious is already 'out of order' - out of the set order of symbolization, out of order like a machine (with its inherent working order) that has been disrupted, overridden, or overloaded. It is crucial then for anyone entering analysis as either patient, analyst, trainee, supervisor, student, or teacher, to address the potential destabilization provoked by confronting unconscious material, including all that is residually unprocessed within it.

*

Pathography - in particular the art of diagnosis - remains central to clinical work in all the 'caring' professions. The main assumption underlying diagnosis - notably the aspiration to capture and control the disease through detailed description - still remains largely unquestioned in everyday clinical practice, despite trenchant critical deconstruction of its *modus operandi* (Foucault,1994). This lack of criticism is not difficult to understand, particularly in the case of analysts working within national and international health systems: it is difficult to remain outside the set politics of differential diagnosis, particularly when national or private insurance companies will fund referral for psychotherapy in some categories of mental disorder (such as depression), but not in others (such as schizophreniform disorders).

Analysts are nonetheless particularly well-situated to observe the inevitable distortions imposed by such categorization. Analysts' own personal analysis (a standard training requirement) may enable awareness of the complex issues encountered in approaching another person's account of their experience: an awareness both of the unconscious dynamics underlying clinical dialogue, particularly transference and countertransference (see Chapter 5) ; and sensitivity to the obtuse, idiosyncratic, and arbitrary development of 'symptoms' associated with mental disorder (see Chapter 3). In this way, analysis must inevitably erode the prognosis, the central diagnostic impulse to control the developmental form of 'symptoms'. In fact, analysis undoubtedly did help disrupt two of the major diagnostic categories of the last *fin de siècle* - hysteria and dementia praecox - whose original distinguishing symptoms subsequently dispersed over a wide spread of differential diagnostic categories, ranging from conversion disorders, to schizophreniform and personality disorders (cf. Roudinesco, 1982).

It is not surprising in this context that clinical work in psychoanalysis has become preoccupied with the main 'out of order' issues of human experience: issues around living alone, facing death, approaching residual psychic pain, and working with loss - including the loss of 'reality' (hallucination and bizarre thought). There are neither set 'solutions' to such issues, nor ready-made prescriptions for better ways to live through them. Analysts really cannot know - and certainly cannot 'cure' - vital unresolved life experiences of their patients: they cannot really enter the intimate terms in which someone split up from a partner, or mourned a parent, or feared the return of murderous or self-destructive fantasies. All they can do instead is to attempt to contain all that pours out from these issues - much of which is necessarily uncontained and uncontainable . This explains both the pivotal role of the notion of containment in contemporary psychoanalytic technique (notably following Bion [1967] and Winnicott [1971]), and the fraught attempts to remove such a notion from any sort of cognitive or interpretative process. Containment implies staying with the symptom in its complex residual form, and refusing reductive interpretative strategies that aim to close down all that is awesome and enigmatic in human experience. As an analyst, you are advised to find your own way to stay with the patient's symptom - not to mention your own identificatory symptom - without resorting to socially and/or medically required 'normalizing' or 'curing' strategies. A patient's flight into health - or his or her discovery of ways to placate clinical and social expectations - can be as short-lived and ultimately self-destructive as the flight into social deviance and so-called perversity. A symptom can return with a revenge after its so-called 'cure', and a chronic disorder can also reinstate itself.

*

What is needed to train someone to be an analyst? The founding fathers and mothers felt that analysts were born rather than trained (cf. Stanton, 1995b, p.93). Appropriate life experience and empathy were regarded as crucial prerequisites, and it was hoped that the extensive personal analysis of analysts would ensure productive contact with any personal weaknesses or blind spots. The requirement of clinical supervision of trainee cases supplemented this, but supervision was neither envisioned as a post-qualification activity, nor as a permanent feature of clinical work. Finally, classes on aspects of the theory and theoretical practice of psychoanalysis were tacked on at the end - or some other appropriate part - of clinical initiation. This part was traditionally labelled 'applied' psychoanalysis, which implied that all that was central to analytic work derived from the clinic.

This tradition of clinical work persists in many contemporary clinical trainings, which maintain in one way or another that too much attention to different theories is confusing - if not dissociating - and that a one-track approach, be it a Balintian, Bionic, Ferenczian, Freudian, Anna Freudian, Groddeckian, Jungian, Kleinian, Lacanian, Laplanchian, Reichian, or Winnicottian approach, is indisputably more containing for future clinicians (cf. Hinshelwood, 1985). It is easy to see the short-term practical advantages in such an approach: it avoids, for example, any obligation to provide thorough and critical examination of differences and tensions between various psychoanalytic traditions; it also intimates that conforming to one school of thought, necessarily obviates a need to forge a truly independent, or individually and critically worked-out place to start clinical work.

Theory is neither particularly autonomous nor particularly unproblematic in relation to clinical work. For Freud, theories emerge as early infantile attempts to make sense of the adult sexual world . The capacity to theorise performs a similar function in the adult world: adults equally turn to theories to construct accounts of all that remains enigmatic in their lives - their unhappiness, their broken relationships, their pain, or their mysterious joys, such as being in love, finding beauty in the world, or falling into an uncanny peace of mind. Such theories intrude right at the start of an analysis, from the very moment a person tries to explain their situation or their difficulties. Normally, the founding problem that brings this person into analysis is that these theories no longer work in practical and visible ways: no matter how many times their set story is repeated, the associated *pathos* [3] persists - they remain depressed, anxious, or in pain.

At this original juncture, both patient and analyst either choose to write off theory altogether, and conclude that even the 'right' theory would not produce catharsis of the associated affect - that 'knowing' why you suffer does not remove the suffering itself; or they conclude that another theory could be more effective, notably a special new theory provided by the analyst. Unfortunately, the latter option remains dangerously seductive for analysts, particularly for those who are trained to follow a single theoretical track. Interpretation then becomes a simple exercise of inducting the patient into the new world of object-relations, structuralist, or post-modern theory. This new theorisation is supposed to privilege and enable the patient to form a 'real' contact with the symptom, thence to dismantle it.

Such a single-track approach ignores the primal structuring of theorisation in the attempt to process enigmatic elements, and locate them somewhere between the outer and inner worlds. Following this primal structure, the process of theorisation inevitably fails, and produces an excess of 'unknown', which we conveniently, if enigmatically, call the unconscious. The unconscious therefore remains integral to the process of theorisation itself, and inevitably installs itself in interpretative narratives at the point where theories fail.

It follows then, that if analysts wish to work at all with such an unconscious, they must also engage with the limits and failures of the 'knowledge' theorisation aspires to provide. In this context, the analyst is indeed placed in the position of one who is 'supposed to know' (to follow Lacan's famous phrase), but it is precisely the limits and failures of this supposition of knowledge that analytical interpretation aims to expose. The analyst's interpretations consequently assume the function of a refusal (Freud's *Versagung*), a refusal to follow the suppositions of knowledge articulated through the patient's theorisation. The analyst simply refuses to follow the story-lines employed by patients to narrate their experience, and always asks for more detail. The analyst equally refuses to supply other theories for the patient - 'hands off the patient's own theorisation', to follow Laplanche's oft-repeated injunction - so that the foundational processes of the theory might emerge (a procedure discussed in detail in Chapter 4).

This view implies a radically different conception of psychoanalytic training. First and foremost, a wide and thorough introduction to theory should become integral to psychoanalytic training, rather than peripheral or 'applied' to it. Central to such training should be special concern for the dangers of set or dogmatic theorisation, particularly in relation to the analyst's own interpretative interventions: like anyone else, analysts unconsciously defend and protect themselves through their interpretations - an issue currently debated under the aegis of 'countertransference' (see Chapter 5).

Secondly, primary concern for the function of knowledge in analysis prompts crucial revisioning of the whole process of psychoanalytic interpretation. Interpretations do not aim to fix or pin down elements of the 'truth' or 'reality' of the symptom, but explore and loosen the complex elements within the constituent narratives. Interpretations are therefore tentative, provisional, and deconstructive. They specifically address issues of narrative detail and so are inevitably small-scale, though they may help to promote the patient's 'constructions' or large-scale accounts of life-experience (see Chapter 6).

Central to this interpretative-constructive process is the promotion of *research* as both an explorative and transformative force in psychoanalytic work [4]. Research vitally involves both the curative and educational impulses underlying psychoanalytic discourse: the patient, like the classical *theor*, is led to explore various affect-laden sites and report back (see Chapter 2); and the analyst must follow the specifics of the analytic discourse into the general narratives that construct everyday life in all its pathology. If analytical interpretations really aim to research the 'out-of-orderness' of symptoms, then they must become street-wise.

If research is taken to be central to psychoanalytic work in this way, then a whole new set of analytical priorities follow: notably, the exploration of thinking, interpretation, and theorisation with all their failures and break-downs (their out-of-orderness); the development of psychoanalytic research in all areas of human thought, culture, and practice - which, in turn, will inevitably transform all the available conceptual tools; engagement with primal experiential research-forms, such as hope and the need to locate 'home' (*Heimat*) [cf.French, 1996]; and the move into interpsychic relational space (looking at dialogic and group structures, for example), as opposed to dwelling with the wilful obscurity of traditional intrapsychic metapsychology (where 'truths' of the 'inner world' remain arcane to each analyst and analysand).

*

This book argues for new approaches to psychoanalytic clinical work in the light of contemporary demands and criticism placed on psychoanalysis. It offers an introduction to the practical issues that arise in clinical work, particularly to the difficulties relating to residual unconscious process - both to the disruptive intrusion of unconscious process in the session, and to the provocation to radical and innovative insight.

There are no recipes for better methods or more efficient work in the clinical illustration here, rather an indication of how clinical experience might inform theory and imaginative construction (in words, pictures, movements, and sounds). In short, this book offers an introduction to the ever present difficulty of staying with - and not rushing to interpret - the raw and complex unconscious material produced in sessions.

The theoretical elaborations here relate to various psycho-analysts and psychoanalytic schools of thought, and particular attention has been given to examination of implications of difference in practice. Particularly challenging, in this respect, is the prospect that the hegemony of insular, single-track, and nationalistic traditions in psychoanalysis might be finally eroded, and replaced by thoroughly and rigorously eclectic trainings that both support analysts in their research of different positions, and enable them to find their own relationship to psychoanalysis.

As the new millennium approaches, it is important that psychoanalysis remains flexible and free-associative in the face of the unconscious, following its founding insights. No doubt, both the function and context of the clinical presence of psychoanalysis will rapidly transform in step with the predictable (and unpredictable) major technological, social and political changes to come. Hopefully, this book might at least suggest some common ground for all who are interested in psychoanalysis about the terms in which analysts might work with such changes.

[1] Samuel Lowy's professional experience included medical and psychoanalytical training in Vienna (where he became a prominent member of the Stekel circle), psychiatric and psychoanalytical work in England (at Manchester Mental Hospital, West London Hospital, and St. Bartholomew's Hospital), and finally clinical and lecturing work in the United States (at the Vanderbilt Clinic of the Columbia Presbyterian Hospital). His clinical books were professional best-sellers in the 1940s and 50s - notably *Dream Interpretation* (1943), *Psychotherapy in the Outpatient Department* (1952), *Transference in Modified Analytical Psychotherapies* (1954) - but he was also generally well-known for his psychoanalytic critiques of contemporary cultural and social issues - such as his wartime classic *Man and His Fellow Men* (1944) and *Cooperation, Tolerance and Prejudice* (1948). Unfortunately his work is now largely overlooked or unknown.

[2] It is important to note in this context that Freud's *Three Essays on the Theory of Sexuality* (Freud, 1905), were centrally involved with *theories* of sexuality, and their function in a child's world (through, for example, the stork stories), and not with some unnegotiable biological notion of innate gender identity.

[3] *Pathos* in Greek indicates the 'suffering' itself, whereas in English use over the last two centuries, the word has tended predominantly to indicate the effect of sadness and pity evoked by written or spoken accounts of suffering.

[4] It is important to note that the promotion of research is common to a wide range of markedly different innovations in contemporary psychoanalysis, e.g. Bion's work on 'thinking'(1962), Lacan's four discourses in Seminar XVII (1991), and Laplanche's theory of translation in Fletcher and Stanton (1992).

CHAPTER 2

THEORY AND SELF-THEORY WITH THE PATIENT

There is a common fear - which is rarely if ever explored in any depth - that some forms of psychoanalysis are too theoretical. It is even sometimes assumed that some forms of analysis are *nothing but theory*, and that the analysand will get little more than a bunch of general abstractions or '*Daily Mail* platitudes about life' (as John Sessions recently characterized the profession in an interview). The perceived theorising tendency is also often pathologized, so 'over-intellectualisation', or a 'tendency to abstraction or to philosophise', are taken to indicate a mental disorder - paranoid psychosis being the most popular, as these diagnostic criteria are standardly applied to it (*DSM4*, p. 287). A friend of mine, an eminent French analyst, told me that he has a standard strategy he employs before speaking to an audience of English or American clinicians, which is to start immediately with a set apology: 'I'm sorry, I'm now going to have refer to theory......it's a French illness, you know...'.

If theory is dangerous or counterindicated in analysis, what is the alternative? In Britain, there is a strong conviction amongst a large section of the clinical community that clinical *observation* is theory-less. This conviction derives considerably from standard psychological testing, and leads to a number of set variables: notably, that the various methods of installing the 'observation' in the session will have no important effect whatsoever on the observed; observing a child/mother interaction, for example, or reviewing videos or tape cassettes of psychoanalytic sessions, will have no input into the process that is being recorded. The 'theory' behind the observation is somehow conceived to be transparent to the 'observed reality'; moreover, the observer is not taken to be included in the observation him or her self. This was beautifully illustrated at a lecture I attended where an analyst was presenting video material which focussed on a child's behaviour in a session, and drew all sorts of 'observational' conclusions from this, before a member of the audience asked why he had not also videoed himself in order to be able to observe the conditions of his own observation. One may well ask similar questions of 'observers' behind the screen in family therapy sessions, or indeed in other group or individual contexts. Of course, these are simple questions which relate to the whole issue of the form and presence of transference in psychoanalytic work in general - but, as we know, some psychologies and psychotherapies ignore transference, others disagree as to its nature, and, finally, the refusal to 'theorize' the issue, and enter into critical discussion about it, further obscures basic features of the analytic context.

Let us look now then at the alternative. First of all, there is no such thing as 'theory-less' psychoanalysis, observation, or anything else. To quote Laplanche: 'Any epistemology or theory of psychoanalysis must take account of the very basic fact that the human subject is a theorizing being and a being which theorizes itself' (1989 p.10) By this, he means that theory is a prime site of experience: 'To state that man is a self-theorizing being is...to state that all real theorization is an experiment and an experience which necessarily involves the researcher' (ibid., p.12-13). Theory is not only a basic way in which we all process experience, but it also implicates both sides of the 'research' that takes place within the psychoanalytic session. To assume therefore that theory pre-exists or simply confirms what happens in psychoanalytic sessions only serves to block the self-theorization of both the analyst and analysand. The effects of this a-theoretical blocking process is nowhere better illustrated than in Lacan's critique of Melanie Klein's *Narrative of a Child Analysis* in *Seminar 1*:'She starts off', says Lacan, 'from ideas which she already has, which are well known...'(Lacan 1988 p.85). So Klein's patient, 'Little Richard', does not have even to play. She apparently knows anyway what is supposed to happen at this stage.

To regard theory as a fundamental process of experience in psychoanalytic work implies a major re-visioning of psychoanalytic technique - and indeed, of the narrative structure in which we construct and report on 'clinical' experience. I use the term 're-vision' here not just in respect to James Hillman (1975), but also to stress the visual component of theory. *Theoria* in the original Latin means 'a wide picture or complete image', which could indeed be made up of 'special images' (like an extended triptych or photo collage of David Hockney). Ruskin recaptured some of this original sense in his use of the term 'theoria' to mean the perceptual (or 'moral') unity in nature as experienced in a landscape (Fuller, 1988). A *Theor* was a person delegated by a community to visit - or rather 'experience' as one now says - holy shrines, and to report back on the effects of this experience to the group. In this sense, it could well be more appropriate to call a patient or analysand a 'theor', because at least the title theor implies personal experiential research at group sites, rather than the subjugation to the scientific or medical gaze implied in the other two terms.

If theory is a fundamental way of processing psychic material, how then does the theor originally come across theory? How also does the theor subsequently work with and assess theory? Freud's *Three Essays on the Theory of Sexuality* set a model for the understanding of the acquisition of theory in the child's *theories* of sexuality; and one should stress 'theories', since Freud's book was not simply about sexuality, but also *theories* of sexuality, and indeed, given the frequent number of later theoretical revisions, Freud clearly regarded the second essay on this subject as central to the whole book. The child's 'theories' of adult sexuality were attempts both to master incestuous and destructive erotic drives, and to de-code the enigmatic sexual messages from the adult world. The ontogenesis of theories in children were therefore primarily related to *desire* [1] - or 'wish' as Strachey translates it - and condensed and displaced in an *epistemophilic drive,* or a drive to 'know'. Here we can see at close range the proximity of ontology (the research of being) and epistemology (the research of meaning) in psychoanalytic theorisation. Ironically, both Lacan and Laplanche are frequently accused of conflating the two - and arguing for the *privilege* of knowledge over being in the psychoanalytic session. This is clearly mistaken.

The child's theorizations - and indeed all our theorizations, if you accept this view - are therefore *complex,* and not transparent to 'reality' or readily reducible to a pre-existent knowledge of reality. Indeed, theory itself produces an unconscious: the attempt to process 'polymorphously perverse' drives and de-code the enigmatic adult sexual messages fails, and leaves an unprocessed enigmatic element. In a remarkable, and, as yet, largely unappreciated study *Stages in the Development of the Sense of Reality,* Ferenczi ([1913]1952) related this failure to process to the hallucinatory dimension of thought to repress the frustration of desire. Thought could not only repeat its process but repress the unprocessed unpleasant or unacceptable. Moreover, it articulated this repression by shifting or removing the visual percepts that caused pain (joy, anxiety, etc.) and installing in their place empty-structure or 'pure theoretical' thoughts. Theories, therefore, in Ferenczi's view, negotiated the problems of 'representability' (cf Freud's reworking of the Kantian *Darstellbarkeit* in the *Interpretation of Dreams*). Theories were the combinatory process of the visual and the cognitive, in which an unconscious excess was produced either through hallucinatory denial (infantile omnipotence) or through unconscious psychic accretion (which he called the teratomic effect).[2]

Theories, then, are not just defences, or indicative of something pathological - though, indeed, of course some theories *may* be pathological - rather they are foundational complex processes of experience. Human beings are primarily self-theorizing. In the context of the psychoanalytic session, it is crucial therefore to support, respect, and pay every attention to the self-theorization of the theor. Theories are not simply delusional, evasive, or self-evident (in so far as they can be empirically verified), but integral parts of a primary creative process. This is well illustrated by a philosophy teacher in Eric Rohmer's film *Conte du Printemps* who explains at length the discovery she has made that everyone has their own philosophy, however crude or sophisticated, and that you cannot touch or attempt to remove this philosophy without losing them altogether. Instead, you have to start with their philosophy and say 'Plato had some interesting things to say too'. Analysis, obviously, is not attempting to *teach* anything like this; but nonetheless, respect for personal forms of theorization is essential for the de-translative and re-translative work which takes place in analysis (we will look at this further in Chapter 5 on Transference).

How then do we work with theories and self-theories in psychoanalysis? First of all - and this issue is widely overlooked - it depends whether we are talking about the analyst's theories or the theor's. Some people imagine, obviously, that Lacan's four graphs of desire, or later the borromean schema, were drawn on the blackboard in his consulting room, and used to explicate the theor's brief productions in the session. Clearly, it is impossible to prevent the theor from reading the analyst's theories - but that is always their reading, and subject to condensations and displacements. Here Lacan's 'clinical interview' in Stuart Schneiderman's edited collection, *How Lacan's Ideas are used in Clinical Practice* (1993) serves as a useful de-translative example of how to deal with such borrowed theorization. In any case, it is important to note and research the analyst's use of theory in the *supervision* session, where the graphs of desire, or Bion's grid, may well serve a different function. But that again depends on researching the nature of interpretation and construction in the supervision, and establishing differences, if any, from the function of theorization in the analytical session itself. I do not wish to go into this further here, but to explore this issue later the Chapter 6 on Interpretation and Construction.

How then to approach the theor's theorization in the analytical session? As I mentioned before, the theor, in early Rome, was delegated to 'experience' the holy sites, and report back on the effect of that experience. What I find useful in this metaphor is the notion of flexible narration of this visit - theorizing, in this sense, as visiting other pre-existent theorizations (parental, familial, social, cultural, or whatever), and de- and re-constructing them. Theorization, in this metaphor, contains *insight* (cf. Hillman (1967); nb.*Erlebnis* in German means 'lived experience'). In this flexible fort/da re-constructive model of theoretical insight, there is no one-track single causal narrative containing the 'meaning' of someone's experience, and no generalisable synchronic closure of that experience either, by which I mean general theorizations like '...but Dads or Mums are like that', which remove the enigmatic and singular nature of theoretical experience.

Finally, if theories - and the singular insights they enable - are complex, they also resist simple or single-track past-present temporalization. They inhabit the a-causal cryptic connections of narratives. In this way, post-Lacanian psychoanalysis is markedly post-modern, as analyst and theor both work through the margins, footnotes, and fragments of pre-existent narratives. It is the enigmatic remains, the unprocessed part of the message which 'naturally' (*pace* Ruskin and his concept of *theoria*) demands further work.

Let us briefly visit (as theors) the case of a woman who was considered a 'dud', notably through having no sense of what to do at school. Her theory - she blamed her father for not 'telling the truth', for being unreal - i.e. it's a fault of the father's theorization. She has no sense of home, and her 9 year old son is terrified by fear of being lost with no map in an open field, and has various nightmares to this effect. She gets him to work on maps. Her mother comes and witnesses this, and wildly - for no apparent reason - accuses her of 'child abuse'. In the account of her relations with her mother, it comes out that her mother's mother had bought the house they live in, and the father had accepted this. Moreover, her mother's mother had never informed her herself of her true father, in fact she had lived under the illusion that her mother's lover had been her father for many years. At this, in the course of a session, this woman arrived at the insight that there was an absent father in her mother's world, and that this father/grandfather to her, had subsequently been suppressed and displaced in the family narrative. Her mother in fact responded to the insight by saying that her father had, in her eyes, been taken in by the 'star' quality of her mother, and had let her mother choose and buy a house for them. This re-theorisation led her to the symptom of her son's anxiety. What here was unprocessed, and where did this symptom come from? In the next chapter, we will look into how the enigmatic is further inscribed in the symptom, and how analyst and theor might work with this.

---

[1] The various distinct uses of the term 'desire' are discussed at length later (see pp.23 &24). It is important to note here, however, that related terms used by Freud - notably, *Wunsch* , *Begierde*, *Lust*, and *Sehnsucht* - have subsequently been interpretatively translated to produce markedly variant uses of the term 'desire' in English and French. First of all, Lacan attempted to re-orientate Freud's usage of such terms around a distinction between the specifics of 'wish' (*Wunsch*) - in which need and demand have a particular object in mind - and the general foundational and unrequitable process of 'desire', which is based on a primal alienation in which 'Man's desire is the desire of the Other' (Lacan 1977 p.235): it is precisely the 'otherness' of desire that constitutes the subject's desire, and its permanent obstruction and ultimate non-recognition. Lacan's engagement with Freud's term *Begierde* (and *das Begehren*) in this context is not particularly appropriate (Lacan 1966, p.690), as, in German, this term connotes the overwhelming passion to consume the 'other' (particularly in sexual and culinary form!). In contrast, therefore, Laplanche has chosen to re-work the related (more poetic) Freudian concept of 'yearning' (*Sehnsucht*), which he has rendered in French as *désirance* : 'it is particularly noteworthy that *Sehnsucht* in no way implies the view of the past, as does the term 'nostalgia' (*Heimweh*), but rather that of the *absence* of the object ... (as

in) the "Sehnsucht of beautiful forests" or the "*Sehnsucht* to see the hour end" (the latter confirming that the term can imply the future as well as the past)' (Laplanche, 1989, p.97).

2 Cf.'Ever since Freud's work, we regard as the fundamental cause of every act of mental representation the wish to put an end to an unpleasantness due to privation, by means of repeating an experience of gratification once enjoyed. If this need is not satisfied in reality, what happens in the first primitive stage of mental development is that on the appearance of the wish [*Wunsch*] (see footnote 1 above) the perception of the previously experienced gratification becomes regressively engaged (*besetzt*) and maintained in a hallucinatory way. The idea is thus treated as equivalent to the reality (perceptual identity, as Freud terms it). Only gradually, sharpened by bitter experience of life, does the child learn to distinguish the wish-idea from real gratification, and to make use of his motor powers only when he has convinced himself that he sees in front of him real objects, and not illusions of his phantasy. Abstract thought, thinking in words, denotes the culminating point of this development. ...Apart from the fact that it takes some time to learn to speak, it seems that speech-signs replacing images, i.e. words, retain for a considerable time a certain tendency to regression, which we can picture to ourselves in a gradually diminishing degree, until the capacity is attained for "abstract" imagination and thought that is almost completely free from hallucinatory perceptual elements.' (Ferenczi,1952,pp.138-139)

CHAPTER 3

RESISTANCE
THE OTHERNESS OF SYMPTOMS

Symptoms are the *primum materium* of medical diagnosis in general, so, to the extent that psychoanalytic psychotherapy operates within a medical context, they also figure prominently in psychoanalytic assessment and 'curative' procedure. Patients or analysands are normally assessed before referral to a psychoanalytic psychotherapist, and the assessment traditionally involves diagnosis along the syndromal lines set out in *DSM 4*, or similar psychiatric manuals. Similarly, the standard psychoanalytic psychotherapy assessment follows set psychiatric procedures for differential diagnosis. It sets out specific symptoms within a syndrome, rates the patient within those parameters, and follows the preponderance of symptomatic features within the syndrome; within *DSM 4*, for example, the weight of rating between listed diagnostic criteria (symptoms) is used to distinguish between diagnoses of Schizophreniform Disorders, Delusional Disorders, Mood Disorders with Psychotic Features, and Psychotic Disorders Not Otherwise Specified (p.303).

In psychoanalytic psychotherapy, as in psychiatry, there is little current speculation on what *constitutes* a symptom, as syndromal categorization is so established. You do hear therapists arguing with a basic diagnosis - suggesting, for example, that someone might not be borderline, schizophreniform, or whatever - but it is rare, given the distinct orders of categorization generally in place. In this sense, current diagnosis lacks the distinction between *symptoms* and*signs* that were integral to medical tradition in the 18th century. As Foucault put it: 'The symptom...is the form in which the disease is presented: of all that is visible....cough, fever, pain in the side and difficulty in breathing are not pleurisy itself - the disease itself is never exposed to the senses, but "reveals itself only in reasoning"...(whereas) the sign announces: the prognostic sign, what will happen; the anamnesic sign, what has happened; the diagnostic sign, what is now taking place...' (*Birth of the Clinic*, p.90). Pulse rate, for example, is a*sign* rather than a symptom, if we follow this distinction.

This distinction between symptoms and signs draws attention to the *problem of symbolization* involved in representing symptoms in the context of diagnosis. To what extent is the very representation of a 'symptom' already constructed within pre-existent diagnostic categories? Or are the same 'symptoms' simply re-aligned within new diagnostic categories as the techniques of diagnosis and treatment become more refined? Symptoms which may well have indicated a diagnosis of 'hysteria' in the 1890s now figure in different diagnostic categories such as conversion disorder or schizophreniform disorder, though, to follow the Foucauldian line, the 'disease' nonetheless remains static within the symptom. The symptom is simply distinguished differently on the level of sign - that is, prognostically, or diagnostically. There are profound - though often unchallenged and uncriticized - implications in this for psychoanalytic work in general, notably concerning which categories of disorder indicate psychoanalytic treatment and which do not. This is particularly the case with schizophreniform disorders, where the absence of a curative prognosis often is taken to counterindicate any 'therapy' at all. As Harold Searles (1992) has put it: what then is one supposed to do with these people, who, after all, constitute one of the largest diagnostic categories of mental disorder? The same question was asked a century ago about hysterics, and psychoanalysis came up with a different reading of the symptom as sign. It seems ironic that we need to go back into such questions to re-examine the relations between psychoanalytic psychotherapy and medical discourse. The sense of the direction of the therapy seems to have got lost.

To repeat: the relation between the symptom and sign poses the question of the status of *symbolization* at play in the symptom. What has been lost is the 'otherness' of the symptom; 'otherness' in the sense that the symptom resists a simple reading as a *sign* of this or that illness or disorder. As Jung cogently stated in 1912: 'psychoanalysis refrains from judging the value of a symptom, and tries instead to understand what tendencies lie beneath that symptom' (Vol.4, p.185). The crucial and revolutionary break that psychoanalysis established with both classic psychiatry and hypnotism was that it did *not* restrict itself to the symptom. Indeed, in an essential way, it *ignored* the symptom. The free associative method led away from the symptom into the complex networks that underlay it. In this way too, psychoanalysis distanced itself from both 'cure' as construed around the 'signs' of the illness, and from 'therapy', in so far as some curative aim (*Zielvorstellung*) is implied in the symptom as sign. As I mentioned before, the psychoanalytic concern for unconscious structure implies both a multiple and complex inscription of psychic process, and a residual resistance of psychic material to translation or conscious representation. Hence there is the original radical shift from 'cure', to *regression* to primal structures; this supposedly brings psychological insight, and promotes psychological depth and quality of life. In so far as the 'otherness' of the symptom can be perceived at all, it has a relation to the complex inscriptions which allow it both initially to be symbolised, and retrospectively re-constructed via free association.

*

Symptoms resist the set direction of the diagnostic signs. What do we mean by this? Lacan theorized this in terms of desire: the symptom indicated a *whole* desire[1], which was rendered complex and fragmentary by the resistance of the subject: 'In order to free the subject's speech, we introduce him into the language of desire, that is to say, into *primary language* in which, beyond what he tells us of himself, he is already talking the unknown to himself, and, in the first place, in the symbols of the symptom' (*Ecrits*, p 81). For Lacan then, the 'otherness' of the symptom is not a quality of the symptom itself, but is introduced in its symbolization - that is, in its engagement with the symbolic networks we have associated with the 'sign'. There is therefore no index of 'regression' in the symptom - regression implying a necessary and complex relation to an original psychic structure - rather there is an indication of the function of language to signify *something quite other* than what it says: not just "disguising the thought" but the function of indicating the place of the subject in the search for the true' (*Ecrits*, p.155). In short, for Lacan, it is the symbolic elaboration of the symptom that renders it 'other', foreign, strange or enigmatic in the directional signs of the body.

Lacan, of course, invokes a 'primary' language of desire here at play in the symptom, by which he literally means a *language*: 'If, for a symptom, whether neurotic or not, to be admitted in psychoanalytic psychopathology, Freud insists on the minimum of overdetermination constituted by a double meaning (symbol of a conflict long dead over and above its function in a *no less symbolic* present conflict), and if he has taught us to follow the ascending ramification of the symbolic lineage in the text of the patient's free associations, in order to map it out at the points where its verbal forms intersect with the nodal points of its structure, then it is already clear that the symptom resolves itself entirely in an analysis of language, because the symptom is itself structured like a language, because it is from language that speech must be delivered' ('The function and field of speech and language in psychoanalysis', *Ecrits*, p.59).

If a symptom is constructed symbolically in its distinction with other symptoms (and overdeterminations), then the symptom is not only a construction of the symbolic but a primary symptom of it. Hence his extraordinary claim that the 'symptom resolves itself entirely in an analysis of language' (ibid.) - language marks the 'otherness' of symptoms in its failure to contain or capture desire.

What I want to take up here is this notion of a primary language of desire somehow pinned down in a symbolic elaboration in the symptom. Is there indeed a primary structure to the symptom, and is it a structure of repression, as Freud and Lacan, in their different ways, would have it? Is this primary structure of the symptom separate from - or even prior to - the symptom as sign with its fixed diagnoses and prognostications?

These questions return to the whole issue of the *complex* structure of the symptom. Complexes, as Laplanche and Pontalis tell us, are the most widely accepted clinical notion deriving from psychoanalysis, but the notion least extensively employed by psychoanalysts themselves (1973 pp. 72-74). Freud himself came to view complexes as 'Jungian mythology', and came to argue by 1914 that the complex is 'a convenient and often indispensable term for summing up a psychological state descriptively. None of the other terms coined by psycho-analysis for its own needs has achieved such widespread popularity or been so misapplied to the detriment of the construction of clearer concepts' (SE.XIV pp.29-30). It is noteworthy here that Freud stresses the *descriptive* value of the complex, description being the primary form classically attributed to the symptom (Foucault, 'The Symptoms as Primary Stratum', op.cit., p.91).

Indeed, following the line of Freud's critique, the complex is often seen as a syncretic and enclosing concept that does indeed indicate a clear diagnosis. This is nowhere better illustrated than in the favourite complexes - the Oedipus and castration complexes - which not only positively prescribe 'normal' development, but also negatively indicate pathology (in the negative Oedipus complex). Interestingly enough, Laplanche extensively critiques this encapsulated notion of the symptom as complex in volume 4 of the *Problematiques* (*L'inconscient et le ça*). He contrasts the Groddeckian 'universalist, infinitist, and totalitarian' view of the symptom - which basically regards the complex and symptom as a transitory illusion - with Freud's approach, which he sees as 'incessantly valorising the limitations of the psychoanalytic method, the limitation of our views, the partial character of our approach, and the necessity to renounce all ambition for universal knowledge, or an exhaustive explanation of the symptom' (p.185). In this view, the symptom is residually complex. Its complexity is marked by its resistance to interpretation, and its irreducibility to fixed diagnosis or prognosis. The symptom therefore remains 'other', it does not disappear, or suddenly 'resolve' in one or other narrative of experience. It is complex, in so far as it is assumed that multiple inscriptions are not 'bound' (*Bindung* , to use Freud's term) or processed in a fixed way. There is no core or nucleus to a complex, but multiple and shifting connections. It is the residual inability to bind the strange, enigmatic, and foreign elements of experience that mark the symptom. Each of our symptoms therefore shifts and transforms rather than disappears, resolves itself, or is 'cured'.

What does this mean clinically? I am clearly not arguing that important disorders are indeed transformed by psychoanalytic psychotherapy, even though, in subsequent chapters, I recount cases where phobias and panic attacks have ceased. I am arguing rather that the associative technique facilitates binding and unbinding processes which facilitate the transformation - or de- and re-translation - of the complex form of experience. The symptom then shifts, like the affect shifts on the surface of the body. How far it shifts, is relative to the extent and form of the complex. This is best illustrated in the somatoform presentation of the symptom - which I would argue is complex and shifting. To give an example:

A Spanish woman in her early 50s whom I saw had suffered a severe paranoid psychotic episode in her 20s which resulted in hospitalisation. She presented recurrent dreams to me of 'operations'... mostly on her body ... her breasts, her womb, then finally cratiotomies - ugly insides to beautiful ones. During the associations she talked extensively about an abusive childhood in which her uncle had tried to touch her up, her breasts, her thighs etc.; then about medicine (she was a doctor), and the non-sexual nature of bodies, which posed her no problems.   It was the pain in peoples' faces she could relate to. Suddenly, the repetitive dreams ended, and she developed intense headaches...which shifted from the eyes to the forehead. She couldn't sleep as a result, but refused to take drugs. She thought she might have a brain tumour, but then reassured herself that it was a 'symptom' - something purely psychosomatic. She started talking about experiences here in Britain during the War when she was a very small child, and she talked at length about bombs. Suddenly she started to sleep again, and had an extraordinary dream in which a bomb hit her road, and her father was dead on the sofa with his legs cut off, and his penis limp and severed as if cut with a knife. She was on the floor and he was at eye level. She thought: he can't walk towards me any more, and she felt this enormous surge of blood into her head which she felt lifted up like a fountain towards the ceiling. But she knew she wasn't dead. At this point she woke up, and her headache had gone. Was she 'cured'? The specific symptom lifted, but she continued to have periodic severe depressions, and became extremely hypochondriacal.

[1] See footnote 1 in Chapter 2

CHAPTER 4

VARIETIES OF SUBJECTIVITY IN
THE CONSULTING ROOM

It is standard strategy in classical psychoanalysis to regard all psychic material that comes up in sessions as products of either the patient's or the analyst's subjectivity. However 'free' the patient's association might be, or however 'arbitrary' the analyst's interpretation, it is still assumed that there is a central conscious focus involved, usually associated with the ego. The analyst and patient are the subject of their expressions in so far as they are assumed to create them. Even in the murky world of compromise-formations and parapraxes in which the subject visibly fails, the creative power of subjectivity is somehow recuperated through the supposed power to redress and marvel retrospectively on the protective and defensive deviousness of the ego (cf. Fenichel,1946,p.578). Hallucinatory and fantasy narratives are likewise categorized in this sense as essentially subjective, and are seen to follow a central narrative order that can be led back through interpretation to less deviant and more creative ego-productions. In short, in this classical psychoanalytic world, there is no other basis for psychic activity in general than subjectivity. The psyche basically works from its own subjective ability to project, irrespective of whether those projections adapt or cohere to the supposed prescribed functioning of either inner or outer worlds.

There is a latent pervasive logic in this view of subjectivity, which, before Lacan, was rarely examined or criticized. First and foremost, the logic implies that everything is essentially *reducible* to subjectivity. Given that the subject is essentially *creative* (even in inverted, destructive ways), psychoanalytic interpretation can creatively repair and restore breaks or infractions of this logic. Furthermore, the primacy of subjectivity - and its projective *modus operandi* - means that it is observable and repairable in its own terms, outside the supposed imposition of secondary cultural, social or specific interpersonal codes. In this sense, the psychoanalyst can conceivably work with and repair the subjective logic of hallucinatory episodes outside - or perhaps *prior* to - the structures that regulate 'normal' social reality. This is certainly what Kleinians intimate when they talk of the 'priority' of the inner world, and argue for an essential primacy of fantasy, projection, and the paranoid-schizoid position as fundamental structures of all human experience.

One damaging effect of this view is to impose a powerful reductive logic in psychoanalytic clinical work in general: everything is reduced to the particular laws and functioning of the given subjectivity, and the fullness and failure of this is taken to be a central focus of the analysis. Even the arbitrary, aimless, senseless, and irrational elements of psychic material are nonetheless taken to have subjective determinants; either negatively, as the dynamics of repression are taken to be essentially subjective (cf. A.Freud, 1946, p.30ff.); or positively, as the unconscious is taken to be essentially a *personal* unconscious, which means that the unconscious structuring of psychic material must at some point follow a specific subjective logic. This explains the bizarre tautologous sense in which such analysts talk about 'becoming aware of' or 'knowing' one's unconscious: as though the personal unconscious is more or less articulable through the specific subjective logic of the patient, it follows that his or her 'awareness', achieved through the analytical reductive logic of their own supposedly personal unconscious production dynamics, will become manifest as a 'deepening' of subjectivity, as opposed to something critical, transcendent or *outside* it.

As simple and attractive as this view of subjectivity may be - because it offers deep understanding of oneself and an untrammelled primacy of the inner world - it is nonetheless deleterious to the essential irreducibility of the unconscious.

Unless an analyst wishes to argue that the unconscious can be 'known', or rendered conscious, then primal unconscious form and process must be essentially unknowable, or unamenable to critique. Similarly, neither the patient nor analyst's 'ego' can become strengthened, nor their sense of subjectivity deepened, through 'knowing' the unconscious. It is rather the failure and limitations of the ego and subjectivity that both mark out the boundaries to residual unconscious material, and form the parameters of psychoanalytic work.

This position is obviously less immediately attractive to ego-orientated analysis - because it offers no clear purposive aim like ego-strengthening or deep-subjectivity - but instead offers something exogenic, which is potentially disruptive, if not deconstructive of subjectivity. In fact, all the essential weaknesses of the classical psychoanalytic position emerge in the attempt to negotiate an impossible integration between the ego and the unconscious. In Klein's case, for example, the ego is taken to be genetically pre-formed and subjectivity is therefore inherited - which implies that the unconscious structure of subjectivity must be essentially biological (Klein, 1975, 2, p.137). Likewise, in Anna Freud's case, an arbitrary and artificial scientific distinction is imposed between general exploration of unconscious structures, which she side-lines as an academic, observational and 'psychological' pursuit, and psychoanalytic *psychotherapy*, in which the unconscious figures therapeutically in a special relationship to the ego (A. Freud, 1946, p 4).

It would be wrong to suggest that Lacan totally escapes the contradictions introduced by this prioritisation of the subject. His extensive critical engagement with the object-relations tradition aims not to discredit its foundation of subjectivity in the 'object' - notably the 'object's' primal psychic function of articulating the instinctual drives of the subject. He is concerned rather with founding the psychic constitution of both the subject and the object in a lack - hence his repeated reference to the more specific concept of the *lack of the object* , as distinct from the more general term 'object relation'. The main effect of this is to question the object-relations location of the real in the 'inner world'. Instead, it is the infant's lack of an 'inner world' way of processing the absence of an object - notably the absence of the mother in the *fort/da* game (described in Freud's *Beyond the Pleasure Principle* [1920]) - that provokes the primal misidentification which founds the subject in a split (Lacan's reading of *Spaltung* [1966, pp. 689-691]). The lack of object therefore structures the subject's entry into the symbolic world. The object itself remains imaginary: its originary lack prevents any permanent capture of the subject's future object-relatedness in either the symbolic world, or in a primary 'real' inner world. Hence the paradoxical and dislocative presence of the imaginary in the Lacanian analytic discourse.

In the Oedipal scenario, for example, the object of castration remains imaginary, and castration is an imaginary lack of an object. Moreover, lack or absence in the real is purely symbolic: an object can only be missing if there is a law which says it should be there. It is crucial for the emergent split subject then to negotiate the law that governs the lack of an object. Lacan's advice here for trainee analysts is to pay particular note to visits to libraries. If you order a book, and are informed that it is not in its place on the shelf, then it is missing *in principle*. The book could well be just a little bit further along the shelf, but this is not the point. For Lacan, librarians have to live entirely in a symbolic world; in contrast, analysts are left to negotiate the remaining imaginary absences in the subject - particularly the frustration and anxiety common both to the analytic session and library research (Lacan, 1994, p.38).

In this way, Lacan opened up two crucial areas of critical enquiry that have radically transformed the perception of subjectivity in clinical work: first, the study of the nature of language; and secondly, work on the concept of 'otherness' as foundational to subjectivity. As far as language is concerned, Lacan established a preliminary distinction between the subject in language - by which he meant subject-positions pre-structured in language which are occupied in speech and writing - and the ego ('le moi' in French), by which he meant an amalgam of fixed identifications, which originated in primary repression. In short, the subject in language and the ego were neither readily assimilable, nor integratable into a unitary subjectivity. On the contrary, the first person singular subject-position in language pre-exists the individual psychological development of ego-function, and, as we know, each child takes some time to stabilize its identification with it, and some indeed never make it [1]. Moreover, the given subject-positions allow multiple and diverse identifications, primarily along different pronominally prescribed tracks (which in some languages incorporate complex social, age, and gender structures). In the clinical context, the great advantage of this approach is to replace a normative developmental view of subjectivity, with a primarily complex, flexible view, that precludes any single or fixed focus. This is particularly appropriate in the study of dissociative identity disorders (multiple personality disorders), in which the various levels of ego structure may be unique, distinct and autonomous, whereas common linguistic subject-positioning can simultaneously be maintained across identities [2].

Lacan's approach to language and subjectivity in clinical work therefore not only radically vitiates the syncretic approach of the classical school, but also questions the supposed curative purpose of language (the 'talking cure') . For Lacan, language comes first, and is not primarily listened to for indications of the health or pathology of the patient's ego. Language is also not scrutinized for its coherence, or narrative ability to 'explain' to the subject the reasons for its distressing symptoms. It is taken rather as complex, fractured, and divested of any ultimate 'meaning' through primary repression. All the language in sessions is therefore subject itself to primary repression, and is either condensed (metaphoric) or displaced (metonymic). Lacanian and post-Lacanian analysts therefore do not wish to treat or 'mend' the supposed manifest symptom in the patient's words, but rather to break words down into more primal complexities. In this, the primal elements - the signifiers or sound and written figurative elements of words - come first, hence Lacan's celebrated encouragement that analysts interpretatively seize the opportunity to metaphorize further and break more words out from any given sound-structure [3]; and also to metonomize further and exploit sound- and visual-connective links (in puns and synecdoche). In this connection, Lacan's advice to prospective analysts that they engage in charades (which means 'conversation' in old French) and cross-word puzzles ('*mots croisés*' or 'crossed words' in French) was not flippant, but intended to promote research into two forms of subjective structure manifest in language: notably the complex and the amalgam .

The second crucial notion that Lacan applied to explore the nature of subjectivity was 'otherness' (l'autre). This term derived from Freud, who used two forms of it '*Der Anderer* ' (the other person) and '*Das Andere* ' (the other thing) to different effect (cf. Fletcher & Stanton, 1992, p.25). In Freud's sense, the 'other person' emitted the message which left a residue in the subject which became the 'other thing'. In contrast, Lacan's use of the terms 'other' and 'otherness' were to indicate the fundamental alienation of the subject. The occupation of a subject-position in language, and subsequent entry into the symbolic order that regulates both subjectivity and communication, was acquired at the expense of a primal identification with the otherness of the world with all its pre-existent *modi operandi*. This alienation, installed through the structural *misrecognition* (*méconnaissance*) of identity between subject and other, was therefore foundational to all experience. In this context, Lacan established a further distinction between a 'small other (object)' (*[objet] petit a*), which referred to the specific alienation of narrative detail, and the 'Big Other' (*le grand A*), which referred to the general alienation of the symbolic order in general.

It is not useful here to explore further the specific conceptualization of this - particularly its relationship to the Oedipus Complex, castration, and the privileging of the phallus and paternal metaphor in Lacanian analysis (cf. Bowie [1991], Boothby [1991], Grosz [1990]), but more germane to observe the specific clinical implications of this notion of alienation in the subject. First of all, it should be stressed that the 'other' for Lacan is an *object* , albeit founded on 'lack'. The object therefore obtrudes as a lack in the symbolization of the representational world. The presence of lack - or, paradoxically, the absence of object - are only established through projective failures of symbolization. The infant's supposed primal projective identification of the lack (of object) with the other subject (the mother/body), patently *fails* to capture and control the mother/body absence in the originary identificatory structure. The identification must fail to coalesce the supposed new subject with the specific lost object (mother/body), and each specific failure punctures a whole in the secondary cohesion of the symbolic: a failure writ large in action - the new subject cannot contain or control the mother/body, presence/absence dichotomies, so they form the basis of a residual unconscious.

In this context, Lacan's initial address to the subject in clinical work is simple and repetitive: it insistently relates back to the primal word-projective-identificatory structure in which the subject originally sets out to master the presence and absence of the mother, or part of the mother's body (the hand, mouth, nipple, breast etc.). For Lacan, prior to the subject's word-projective identification with the other - and its subsequent fundamental alienation in - lies unconscious dislocated sensory experience, which insinuates and disrupts the body's somatic processes. Initially, Lacan freely and imaginatively borrows from Klein, and regards *imagos* - or culturally inherited unconscious visual and/or auditory structures - as the main articulation of this primal experience: he elaborates extensively on the imago of the mother's body: '... through this', he explained, '...we have the cartography of the child's inner world drawn by their own very hands, and we have the historical atlas of intestinal divisions, where the imagos of real or virtual fathers and brothers articulate the subject's voracious aggression in fighting for deleterious hold over the sacred regions of her body' (Lacan, 1966, p.115). These imagos re-emerge in regressive fantasies of evisceration, chopped up or broken up bodies (*imagos du corps morcelé*), which commonly feature in psychotic episodes. Later Lacan moves on to more complex theorizations of trapped, non-processable areas within figurative and written discourse, notably in connection with the *sinthome* (an archaic spelling of the French word symptôme). This concept is explored primarily through engagement with James Joyce's epiphanic writing and Jacques Derrida's critique of the Lacanian 'agency of the letter' in *The Post Card* (Lacan, Seminar XXIII 'Le Sinthome' [1972]; Derrida [1987]; Stanton, in Stanton & Reason [1996]; Thurston, in Stanton & Reason [1996]).

Post-Lacanians - particularly Laplanche - have followed Lacan's general clinical focus on 'otherness', but questioned the specifics associated with the (small) 'other' object, and its projective engenderings. Instead, Laplanche argues for an absolute priority of the other - by which he means first and foremost the priority of the other person - over the subject. For him, the subject emerges through attempts to process the messages that come from the other person. Such attempts bind and pin down elements of this message (in what Laplanche calls a 'translation'), but miss and fail to process other elements, which then persist in their unprocessed state as 'unconscious' . The unconscious is thus seen as an excess of the untranslated or unprocessed elements of the message from the other person; Laplanche calls it the 'à traduire' - the 'to be translated' - which is structurally foundational to the unconscious.

The absolute priority of the message from the other person necessarily implies a radical reconceptualization of both the role of subjectivity, and its function in psychoanalysis. Above all, the central focus of the analytical session shifts from the projective capacities of the subject to what comes through the subject from the other person. It is then a question of establishing what remains unprocessed behind the set narrative translations of experience brought by both the patient and the analyst.

The principal subjective psychic process therefore is no longer projection but introjection; and introjection is defined as the process through which which subjectivity establishes itself in attempts to translate messages that are implanted by the other. Moreover, through this introjective process, subjectivity progressively generates its own fixed points and agencies (the ego, ego-ideal, ideal-ego, and super-ego[4]). The foundational heterogeny of these agencies means that they can never be set up as transcendent - in the sense of containing some transparency into their own or other psychic function - but instead need to be approached as complex and multiply determined.

In this context, the priority of introjection has a particularly radical effect on the conception of the ego. As the implantation of messages from the other precedes the emergence of ego function, and indeed precedes the subject's acquisition of language, the origins and primal structure of the ego are neither psychologically self-contained (or self-regulated) nor essentially linguistic. Instead, the first messages from the other are processed in a sensory way as affects. The introspective process fixes these affects on the body, and gradually coheres this range of affects into a body-surface, the skin, which subsequently facilitates the subjective distinction between a psychosomatic inside and outside to affects.

The first prototypical ego is therefore a bodily ego, or what Laplanche calls a 'body-source'. But unlike Anzieu and Bick, who have similarly talked about the skin as the first containing body-ego, Laplanche regards this body-ego not as a first projective vector, but as essentially introjective (Laplanche, 1993). The first intake of messages from the other is neither naturally assimilated, nor greeted with projective elaboration, but experienced as an intrusion of the other. The affective processing of the inside of the body is therefore also primally marked out as 'other' - the inner body is therefore an 'inner foreign body' (*corps étranger interne*) (Laplanche, 1993).

In the clinical context, this leads to the crucial issue of the nature of affects or 'feelings', and their relationship to subjectivity. What does it mean to have *feelings* ? To what extent can we *own* or *control* such feelings ? What role does the body play in feelings? Does our body-pleasure or body-pain *ventriloquize* (to follow Ferenczi's notion of '*Bauchreden* ') our psychic processes, or is it the other way round? Such basic questions frame both what we take as 'subjective' in the analytical session, and the ways in we propose to work psychoanalytically with such subjectivity within the session. For classical analysts, of course, the main problem is with the body. The body is immobilised on the couch, albeit often in a suggestively erotic way, and the analyst is forbidden to touch the patient in any way whatsoever (Peyru, 1992; Casement, 1985). Everything therefore is communicated through language. The body then figures principally as part of the symbolic order, subject to the same projective elaborations, and metaphoric and metonymic re-processing, as everything else. The problem here is twofold: first, as we have seen, language is not primary to the body-sourcing of the ego; and secondly, the ego neither 'invests' the body with feeling, nor is able fundamentally to alter the alienation (or otherness) of body-affects.

This is particularly evident with somatoform (or psychosomatic) disorders, where false distinctions between psychogenic and biogenic pathologies can be fatal [5]. Of course, it need not necessarily be one or the other, and may well indeed be both: the symptoms must also necessarily be complex and multiply-determined. For example: the case of a patient who brought a dream of his head catching fire - a dream which occasioned numerous associations. The patient was later discovered to have a malignant brain tumour from which he died. In fact, despite obvious inferences, the discovery of the tumour neither vitiated previous (supposedly unrelated) associations, nor established a clear causality in which the dream image was the result of the organic illness or vice-versa. Indeed, the main problem arises precisely when it is asked whether psychoanalytic clinical work should or could aim to 'cure' such observable symptoms. This aspect of the 'otherness' of symptoms was discussed in Chapter 3.

*

How then is it possible to work with these residual unprocessed 'other' elements trapped in both the analyst's and patients' (inter)subjectivity? It is striking how often the stories from both sides of the couch return to the enclosing but impenetrable narrative of the other person. For patients, familiarly, the parental or family story is deeply engraved in great and exact detail, but there seems to be no personal way into the narrative in order to be able to unpack it and make up one's own account of it. For the analyst, in contrast, there is the set regression pre-structured in the 'omnipotence' of the analytical position, which enables the technical power of theories (and implicit identification with their originators) to miss out major bits of unprocessed material and still claim 'knowledge' of a symptom [6]

A woman in her late 40s came to see me complaining of

unbearable depression and 'loss of identity'. She was a social worker who worked with delinquent adolescent women. She had become chronically insomniac, sleeping only an hour or so a night. She refused medication, and found it increasingly hard to get up in the morning. It was particularly hard for her to get her legs to move, and she often experienced a sense of heavy weight around her pelvic region. She married her first lover whom she had met at university, and they had four children together - two boys and two girls. Her husband was an ambitious engineer, and moved the family around frequently in order to advance his career. He was absent for long periods of time, and she became lonely and frustrated. She had a couple of brief sexual affairs with men at work that she 'hardly noticed'; the only effect they had on her was to confirm to her that she was 'an inadequate mother' - 'inadequate' because she spent the time on these 'pointless' affairs rather than staying at home with her children. Twelve years into her marriage, she discovered that her husband had conducted numerous affairs since they had met. She was shocked that she had had no idea of what had really been going on. She packed her bags, took her children, and twelve years later came to see me. She said that she had come to see me both to mourn the death of her marriage and her failure as a mother; in her view, both these issues lay at the heart of her depression.

The first few months of the analysis focussed on the theme of mourning - not the mourning of her marriage as she had initially mentioned, but the mourning of her parents who had been killed in a car accident fifteen years earlier. She arrived at every session (four sessions a week) dressed in black, and talked at great length and impassively about the 'arbitrary' and 'impromptu' nature of the loss of her parents - though it was clear that she felt that the accident had some deeper significance. Her main concern was that she had 'felt nothing' - except she had realized on several occasions that she had been 'unusually depressed' on the anniversary date of the accident.

Initially, she accounted for the absence of feeling in terms of her overwork and lack of time, but this line of thinking appeared increasingly inadequate to her after each repetition.

I asked her about her family's response to the accident. She seemed surprised by the question, and forcibly dismissed it as 'irrelevant' because her two much older brothers lived on 'opposite sides of the globe' (one in Singapore and the other in Los Angeles). She then dismissed the whole family as 'autistic'. I asked her what she meant by this word, and she apologized for being 'scientific', but suggested that, in my profession, I should know what the word meant.

She then told me that, for her, the word meant 'emotionally dead'. When I asked her if she included herself in this family description, she flared up in great anger, and then dissolved in tears.

Henceforth, she lost the deadness and impassivity of the early sessions, and became regularly extremely angry about a whole range of people and everyday issues. She put this down to 'new-found sensitivity and vulnerability', though she still complained vehemently that these strong feelings had not enabled her to recover any of her 'loss of self'. She had just become more sensitive to the fact that she was a victim who was 'daily deadened' by life around her. She sobbed through two months of sessions , which she later called her 'tearful stage'. Throughout this time, she refused my offer of paper tissues, and made a point of bringing her own supply. Despite this insistence on her own ability to look after herself, she still felt utterly powerless and 'unfeeling'.

At this point, her depression and insomnia became markedly worse. She experienced repetitive short hallucinations of white forked lightning flashes, as well as a narrowing of her visual field into a single vertical strip. She was terrified of losing her sight - a condition she believed was the inevitable 'genetic consequence' of her loss of subjectivity. She started to wear dark spectacles all the time, even at night, for fear of the lightning. She started to report and recount a large number of dreams, even though she felt she was not sleeping at all, and could not distinguish between dreams, fantasies, and hallucinations. Her dreams were all about dead, and often limbless, headless, or 'gnawed' bodies floating in an underground stream; in later dreams, the stream was consistently a Victorian sewer, though in one significant variant, she discovered that the liquid was blood, filled with large coagulated bits, rather than the usual urine and faeces.

The main associations which emerged around her account of these dreams concerned a repeated event in her childhood. Often, when she was in the toilet, someone would lock her in, and turn off the light. They would leave her there for hours, even though she could hear voices in conversation in the nearby living room. The voices never replied to her shouts and pleas, so she always felt herself fall into the silence and darkness. Even her wild thoughts about being locked in forever, or being attacked by some stranger or rat, ceased, and she stopped smelling the mix of urine and faeces which permeated the place (as the toilet was never cleaned). Eventually the door would be quietly unlocked. On her return to the living room, all the family continued talking to each other as if nothing had happened. Despite her obvious distress, they all refused to discuss the incident.

It was an important breakthrough for her to connect her lack of a 'sense of self' with 'being in the dark'. My own sense of the direction of the work here was to enable her to unpack and explore all that was tied up with darkness. Basic questions arose: who had locked her in? why did they do it? what sounds and scenes filtered in from the outside? These questions actually served to reinforce the darkness, because they only further confirmed the fact that she did not know: she did not know who had locked her in, though she had a strong intuition that it was her father; she never knew why she was locked in, but was plagued by intrusive thoughts that she had done something wrong (though she knew that she had not); and, finally, she could not make any overall sense of the world on the other side of the locked toilet door, other than that she was excluded from it.

Nonetheless, this exploration of aspects of the darkness enabled her to identify different potential stories 'out there' that, in one way or another, conspired to lock her out of their world. It was vital for her to realize that the other people were not looking at her at all. When she came back to the living room, they were all tied up in their own particular scene. She came to see this as both a relief, and a way out of the darkness, because she no longer had to construct a picture of herself from the 'otherness' of her experience; neither from the bizarre snippets of information gleaned from 'autistic' family gatherings, nor from the hallucinatory visual and auditory fragments magically endowed with terror (particularly the faeces, urine and blood in her dreams, and the lightning/light-turned-back-on of her hallucinations).

She now began to sleep better, though fitfully, but her pelvis had 'stiffened', and she still found it difficult to walk. She also told me that she had started to draw herself as a way of 'letting out more of the new "me"'. She brought one crayon drawing of herself, dressed in very baggy black trousers. The top part of her body was simply outlined, but she had coloured in her breasts in white, and her nipples in vivid red. Her main associations around this drawing concerned her mother. She recalled that she had never seen her mother naked, and had no recollection of her mother ever holding her. The only physically intimate moments between them occurred after her brothers had left home. Her mother used to put her head in her daughter's lap, and talk about the past. The mother would sob out and repeat the same story of how violent her father was, and how she dreaded going to her bedroom as a child in case she had to pass her father who would frequently expose his erect penis.

My patient's main feeling about this story was that she had no way into it: it was always told in exactly the same way, and if she asked questions, the details would simply be reiterated. On the one hand, it seemed enormously productive to 'get out of the darkness' by assuming her mother's position in an other (outside) story; on the other hand, it was profoundly claustrophobic to experience the lack of narrative space in that story; she complained it was like moving from a large dark toilet into a smaller 'dazzlingly lit' one.

This explorative shift into her mother's position also provoked extreme frustration and anger. She became convinced that there was another more important 'secret' hidden in her mother's story, and that, somehow, this secret explained the unspoken hostility between her mother and father, which in turn generated the family 'autism', and her own exclusion. But she now felt certain that her own efforts would unlock this secret . For the first time she started to talk about 'a sense of me', and a corresponding sense of personal agency. She started to learn Welsh - her mother's mother-tongue - as a part of this new sense of purpose. This had important resonances for both of us, as she had discovered from a dedication in one of my books that my deceased mother was also Welsh-speaking. This led her to hypothesize wrongly that I understood Welsh - the mothers' language - but my refusal to confirm this was only met with disbelief: 'how could one not understand one's own mother's tongue?' she insisted. I took this as a measure of the depth of her adhesion to psychoanalytic ways of working, and of her precarious overvaluation of them.

She continued to have brief hallucinatory experiences of lightning, but these suddenly became connected to 'flashbacks' (as she called them) of her father's sexual abuse of her. She remained deeply unsure whether these incidents were 'real' - a doubt she never had about the flashes of lightning. She was particularly troubled by the fact that the flash-back incidents all involved the exposure of her father's erect penis - a scene she had never recalled before, but which was now indissolubly linked with her mother's story. She felt no need whatsoever to resolve this doubt. It had now become totally unimportant to determine whether the sexual abuse was 'real'. Instead it was essential to explore the nature and extent of her own damage. Indeed, she felt compelled to 'claim back' good aspects of her/the father from her mother's story, and even reverted for a while to using her father's surname.

It would be easy to identify elements of 'cure' in this brief account: her mobility problems eased significantly after her location of the weight of her mother's head on her lap; she developed a 'sense' of her own physical presence and alert- ness, and started to wear different and complexly coloured clothes; and she also began to feel that she 'owned' her own depressive periods. But my main point in discussing this case is to illustrate how the big shifts that occurred in her analysis were directly related to her engagement with 'otherness'. This occurred first when she connected her 'loss of self' with 'being in the dark'; and later, after she had explored the 'oth- erness' of her mother's position, she was able to relate the claustrophobic elements of her own 'loss of self' with the lack of interpretative space in her mother's stories. Most important of all, these connections enabled her to get into and shift 'uncontrollable' elements in her hallucinatory and somatic experiences: the 'abstract' and visual-frame-shifts of the light- ning hallucinations became attached to concrete delusional 'flash-backs' of sexual abuse - which provided her with an alternative framework in which to distinguish fantasy and 'real' aspects of experience within her own subjective space; secondly, she was enabled through her exploration of the spe- cific points where she was barred from entry into her moth- er's story, to see the precise somatoform location of the unprocessed elements of that story on her own body. The 'other' unknown side - her mother's sobbing head - was returned to the symptom of her pelvic 'heaviness' and loss of motility.

[1] It is a moot point whether autistic people possess subjectivity in this sense.

[2] In some cases of dissociative identity disorder, for example, there are specific somato-form connections - for example, a patient's different identities can have different eyesight prescriptions (cf. *DSM4*, 1994, p.485, 'associated laboratory findings').

[3] cf. Freud's 'Signorelli' example, and Lacan's account of it.

[4] Although Freud draws no clear conceptual distinction between the 'ideal ego' (*Idealich*) and the 'ego-ideal' (*Ichideal*), some analysts have subsequently argued that such a distinction might indeed serve important purposes. Nunberg ([1932] 1955), first of all, suggests that the ideal ego is a separate entity and forms prior to the superego; thus it is less differentiated and more omnipotent than the ego-ideal, which engages with later superego prohibitions. Lagache later explores the clinical implication of such a distinction in the specific context of identity disorders: 'In analytic experience, even in the case of subjects fixed in the naive belief in their identity, the question is raised, "Who am I?" or "What am I?" - my * or the refusal of it? adult or child? man or woman? ,master or subject? These latter alternatives relate most significantly to internal conflicts of identifications: they raise the problem of the subject's choice between the ego ideal and the ideal ego, the ego ideal responding to the expectations of the authority internalized in the superego, and the ideal ego to a narcissistic and domi-nating position in which fantasies of omnipotence are supported by identification with the patient, him- or her- self represented as omnipotent' (Lagache, 1993, p.247). Directly follow-ing Lagache, Lacan further elaborates this distinction to speculate how the ideal ego might function in omnipotent fantasy intrusion, particularly in psychotic episodes: he suggests it is crucial, in this context, '... To image how the relation to the mirror, which establishes the imaginary relation to the other and the capture of the ego ideal, serves to lead the subject into a field where it hypostasizes itself as the ideal ego' (Lacan, 'Remarque sur le Rapport de Daniel Lagache', 1966, p.680).

In contrast, other contemporary analysts have chosen to ignore this added distinction: Janine Chasseguet-Smirgel, for example, writes that 'For my part I have not judged it neces-sary to distinguish between ego-ideal and ideal ego, in as much as any study of the ego ideal implies a study of the different forms that the attempt to recapture lost narcissism may take' (Chasseguet-Smirgel, 1985, p.245).

[5] This is particularly the case with patients referred to psychotherapists with depression, who in fact have an undetected organic illness. It would be good to think that psychothera-pists would be able to detect this, but this is too often not the case.

[6] It is interesting here that Jung initially suggested that all issues of clinical technique should address the *'feeling-tone'* of complexes of ideas (Jung, 1961, 4, p.26).

CHAPTER 5

THE TRANSFERENCE
DE-TRANSLATING THE MESSAGE

It is important to stress, right at the start, that there are radical differences between French and Anglo-American
approaches to transference. This difference has remained
remarkably politically divisive between these two psychoanalytic traditions, though, so far, the French have proven much
more ready to enter into debate with protagonists than the
Anglo-Americans. It is significant, for example, that the
'transference' section of Sandler, Dare and Holder's text-book
is at pains to draw attention to relatively minor conceptual
differences within the Anglo-American School, but totally
ignores the major differences with the main French conceptualizations elaborated by Lagache, Lacan, and Laplanche
(Sandler, Dare & Holder, 1979, pp. 43-45). This omission is
particularly significant in the context of the political conflict
which emerged between 1951-1954, which both engendered
an independent French tradition around the foundation of the
Société Française de Psychanalyse in 1954, and isolated
Lagachian, Lacanian and Laplanchian thought in this field
from the mainstream of the International Psychoanalytical
Association (IPA). Although Lagache and Laplanche were
both later reintegrated into the IPA, it remains doubtful
whether their thought on transference has yet been taken seri-
ously within classical non-French clinical trainings.

In contrast, French conceptual elaborations of transference
have readily critically engaged with Anglo-American coun-
terparts. Two central 'position documents' written during the
1951-1954 conflict - namely Lagache's 'Some Aspects of
Transference'(1951) [Lagache, 1993], and Lacan's 'Intervention
on Transference' (1952) [English version in Mitchell & Rose,
1982] - both focus on the shortfall of Anglo-American ego-

psychological and object-relations approaches to the subject. Lagache trenchantly criticized Anglo-American approaches for 'culturally generalizing' the notion out of any clinical specificity, and also for excising Freud's rooting of transference in the *spontaneity* of the clinical session (Lagache, 1993, p.140); Lacan aimed to expose a fundamental epistemological conceit behind the Kleinian prioritization of a notion of countertransference, which he believed delusionally inflated the power of the analyst's 'knowledge' of the impact of the patient on the analyst's own transference, and attempted to remove all the primal unprocessed, unfinished, and untranslatable elements originally incorporated in Freud's interpersonal notion of transference (Lacan, 1991, *Seminar VIII: Le Transfert* pp.223-231).

What then are the broad and fundamental differences involved between Anglo-American and French definitions of transference? First of all, following the French tradition, transference is taken to be a primary phenomenon which pre-structures all communication, including the psychoanalytic exchange. In this sense, transference is the primary unconscious process which places the subject in the position to communicate in the first place; that is, the identification of (an)other to communicate with, which, of course, in the Lacanian framework, implies a primary *misrecognition* that allows the subject to pose itself as 'other': 'Every discovery of one's own unconscious presents itself as a stage of a translation in progress of an unconscious which is above all an unconscious formed of otherness ...this enables us to know (savoir) the essential element of my teaching ... the positive power of misrecognition' (Lacan, ibid. p.218).

Transference therefore not only articulates sense and meaning, but also the primary repression needed to maintain the sense and meaning of communication with that 'other'. In short, transference preserves the effect of 'knowledge' of the other - knowledge which is amplified in the psychoanalytic encounter in the 'other person' of the analyst, whom Lacan intriguingly entitles 'the person who is *supposed* to know' (the accent being on *supposed*).

The corollary of this view is that transference only becomes manifest when this 'knowledge' fails to reveal the primary complex and repressed structure of the act of communication itself - namely when the residual 'otherness' of the other object or person intrudes upon the illusion of transparency or 'knowledge of' the other. In the analytic context, this is when the analysis stalls, identifications fail, and the 'knowledge' of the analyst simply excoriates the alienation of the analysand.

This crucial observation initially leads Lagache to insist on a clinical distinction between 'transference neurosis' - which is uniquely generated by the 'frustrating, infantile, unreal aspects of the analytic environment...that produce transference regression' - and 'general transference' which is practically uneliminable in human relationships (Lagache, 1993, p.140 & p.144). This distinction is taken up and developed further within the Lacanian and post-Lacanian tradition: transference-neurosis occurs in analysis when the analyst, in the patient's communications, returns to being 'other' in more primal, infantile, intrusive and foreclusive ways. Powerful and uncanny preverbal material infuses into the analysand's symbolic world, and renders it increasingly fragmentary. This inevitably subverts the position of the analyst's supposed 'knowledge' of the patient, and so dramatically brings to an end any effects of 'transparency of knowledge'. For Lacan, this is precisely what happened to Freud in his analysis of Dora - 'the first case in which Freud realized that the analyst played his part' (Lacan, 'Intervention on Transference', in Mitchell & Rose, 1982, p.64.). The crucial issue for the analyst then is not to persist in 'knowing' how to try and interpret the transference; rather, it is in developing ways of working *in* the transference which address the primal preverbal material it presents.

If we accept this view of transference, it is no longer *stricto sensu* possible to interpret the transference, as many Anglo-American analysts claim to do. Transference does not facilitate clarity - clarity of interpretation - but, on the contrary, promotes the foundational structure of otherness. Transference resists interpretation and *insists* in the communication with others. This is why transference emerges in the stallings of communication in analysis, and insistently installs itself communicatively through repetitions. In this context, transference does not operate the repetition of numerous unresolved infantile conflicts (as Freud initially intimated in his 1912 paper 'The Dynamics of Transference'), but rather a *specific and structural need to repeat* (cf. Lagache, 1993, p.137). For both Lagache and Lacan, this specific repetitive structure of transference is installed by a primal narcissistic injury to the ego by the intrusion of the other (person and thing) into the libidinal flow. In this, the ego is not only 'ripped' or 'split' (the Freudian *Ichspaltung* or the Lacanian *refente* [Lacan, 1966, p.842]), but is permanently marked by a 'dangerous and humiliating privation' (Lagache, 1993, p.138). In the spontaneity of transference, therefore, the ego is restrained by these primal cuts, marks, and privations. It can no longer process and connect the effects of the communication, nor can it repair the visible damage to its own operation. So the subsequent ego-effects of incompleteness and failure actively further the path of repetition-compulsion in transference. Lagache, followed by Lacan, labelled this the *Zeigarnik Effect* , to evoke Zeigarnik's 1927 experimental discovery that unfinished or failed tasks are much more often recalled than completed or successful ones (Lagache, 1993, pp.116-117; Lacan, 1966, p.215).

This view of transference imposes crucial critical revisions. Above all, it suggests that transference operates primarily introjectively: 'other' elements intrude, distort, dislocate and damage the communicative operation of the ego. This vitiates the projective (or projective identification) conception of transference which relatively and negatively empowers the ego: the kind of transference interpretation, for example, which typically argues that the patient is not really addressing the analyst but the mother, father, or sibling, suggests that the form and content of the communication remain unchanged and accurate, and only the 'object' or 'aim' of the communication becomes dislocated. In fact, such transference interpretation simply multiplies the complex elaboration of the original transference, and thus intensifies the underlying repetition-compulsion. Such multiplication and intensification is enhanced to a further degree by so-called countertransference interpretation. To suggest, for example, that images raised in a patient's dream might actually operate a countertransferential exchange from patient to analyst - that is, to propose an essential latent communication from patient to analyst - in effect removes the patient a further step away from addressing the residual otherness of the dream. In fact, the (counter)transference structures precisely all that is *not* symbolically processed and ego-integrated in the dream-image and (re)presentation.

*

Laplanche's substantial revision and contribution to this tradition, is based first of all on an alternative reading of Freud's term *Lösung* - which is translated by Strachey as the 'resolution' or 'dissolution' of transference, and subsequently adopted by generations of analysts to support the view that transference can be interpreted away. In contrast, Laplanche has suggested that the non-resolutive senses of the term - notably loosening, slackening, unbinding, and relaxing - are more appropriate to transference (Laplanche, 'Of Transference', 1993[a], p.421); and, moreover, that these senses are reinforced by Freud's repeated use of the related terms *ablösen* (to loosen, unloose. scale off, or sever), *auflösen* (to loosen, untie, unravel, reduce, or decompose), and *erlösen* (to redeem or to release) [ibid. p.434]. If transference residually and unconsciously underlies human communication, then analysis cannot 'resolve' the transference - a dangerous position for analysts to adopt anyway, given the definitive role transference plays in analytic work (Laplanche humorously compares this position to analysts sawing off the tree-branch on which they are sitting [1993(a), p.421]). It follows then - if there cannot be an analysis *of* the transference, only an analysis *in* the transference - that psychoanalytic work should aim rather at a loosening or unbinding (*Lösung*) of it. This cannot dissolve transference as such, but aims to make a specific transference change modality.

In this context, Laplanche's introduction of two distinct modalities of transference - the embossed transference (*le transfert en plein*) and the hollowed out transference (*le transfert en creux*) - adds a new dimension to analytic work in the transference. In an embossed transference, the unprocessed unconscious material transferred from the other person blocks symbolization. In traumatic communications between parents and children, for example, the unconscious unprocessed material transferred from the adult to the child in a violent or sexual intrusion will become 'embossed': it will obtrude in all compulsive repetitions of the transference, particularly and dramatically in the 'unreal' context of the analytic encounter. There may be no apparent way associatively to 'loosen' the hold of a particular image, or the tight compulsion of a given narrative of an event (including so-called 'flashback' detail), in which case the transference will stall.

Alternatively, associative and interpretative work might provoke the unbinding (*Lösung*) of embossed components of the transference. The somatic and affective charge of the transference will then experientially decrease - it will be increasingly 'hollowed out' (*en creux*). Laplanche's notion of this 'hollowing out' process is that it effects a return to an original transference-structure - the hollowed out transference (*le transfert en creux*) - where a primal enigmatic relationship to the otherness of the unconscious, re-inspires a drive to process all that appears enigmatic, other, and unprocessed. In short, the more the 'embossed' and unprocessed elements in transference are loosened through association and interpretation, the more space will be 'hollowed out' for the patient, which in turn affords more freedom and release (*Lösung*) to address other unprocessed material.

Of course, Laplanche is well aware of the problems and awkwardness of this formulation: particularly the difficulties in accounting dynamically for returns and rebounds from the 'hollowed out' to the 'embossed' modalities of transference; as well as the practical problem of distinguishing a primal relationship to the 'enigmatic' from the more embossed forms encountered in most of everyday clinical life (cf. Laplanche, 1993[a], p.417)

Nonetheless, he initiates crucial exploration into transference modes of unprocessed material, which are particularly important in approaching the transgenerational transmission of traumatic material. In the last decade, there has been extensive on the impact of major group traumas such as the two World Wars, the Holocaust, exile, and natural disasters, on following generations (Eickhoff [1989], Kestenberg [1993], Luel & Marcus [1984] and Wangh [1968]). Research on delusional and bizarre-thought material produced in psychoanalytic sessions has also indicated the generational transmission of specific images and somatoform responses: unprocessed material, for example, produced in psychotherapy sessions with anxiety-disordered German teenagers, has been traced back to grandparental experience (Ehlers & Crick 1994); similarly, in Israel, distinct forms of somatoform and delusional PTSD response in relatives of holocaust survivors have emerged in official research (most recently in the study of widespread anxiety disorders provoked by the issue of gas-masks during the Gulf War [University of Tel Aviv Research Reports]).

Laplanche has introduced a translation model to explain the generational transmission of symptoms in the transference. First of all, he suggests that it is fundamentally significant that Freud uses the two terms 'translation' (*übersetzung*) and 'transference' (*übertragung*) interchangeably (Laplanche, 'The Wall and the Arcade', in Fletcher & Stanton, 1992, p.201; cf. Freud, *Interpretation of Dreams*, 1900, pp. 339-341 and *Die Traumdeutung* , pp.335-337). In the process of translation, specific elements of meaning are 'transferred' from one language to another but something is always missed. For Laplanche, the patient's attempt to 'translate' their experience misses elements that remain residually untranslated. The analyst's interpretations 'loosen up' (*lösen*) the specific elements of these translations - a process which enables the patient to 'de-translate' previous translation-attempts. In the course of de-translation, the patient is not only empowered to re-translate, but also to 'hollow out' some unprocessed material that is 'embossed' in the transference. Obviously, as with all translation, there will remain a residual untranslated area which will continue significantly to structure the transference. Laplanche refers to these as 'psychotic enclaves' - which he believes operate along similar lines to taboos (cf.Laplanche in Fletcher & Stanton, 1992, pp.11-12). Psychotic enclaves, like taboos, assume specific collective characteristics through the detailed shaping of wars, natural disasters, and severe social and familial crises. They are sensorially and somatically encrypted, and provoke 'embossed' responses in the transference: such as the responses to gas masks during the Gulf War, or the panic-attack a patient of mine experienced during a session when a siren went off outside - an effect she could only relate to childhood experiences in the 1950s when she thought sirens announced both a nuclear war and her parents' immediate panic and collapse, which they explained (unconvincingly to her) was due to their experience of the bombings of London during the Second World War.

*

The following case illustrates both transference-stalling and the way in which de-translation of emergent unprocessed psychic material may shift (but not remove) the modality of the transference. The patient - a woman in her mid-thirties, from a 'good English aristocratic family' - was referred to me by a couple of marital therapists whom the woman and her husband were consulting about 'relationship problems'. In their referral report, the marital therapists advised that the woman was 'forceful and uncooperative', and that she refused to take on board any issues raised either by her husband or themselves. According to them, the husband was 'henpecked and compliant', but wished to continue the relationship at any cost; the wife seemed 'cool if not icy' about the marriage, but surprisingly remained 'adamant to make things good'. The therapists had a doubtful prognosis for the marriage, and were even more doubtful about the woman's suitability for psychoanalysis.

From the first session, she was both aggressive and suspicious of me. She suggested initially that I would never be able to understand her aristocratic family background. A few sessions later, she suddenly apologized for this, mentioning that she had checked up on my qualifications, and noted that I had studied at Oxford University, so I 'must know some people like her'. But she started the next session with a new fear that I would not understand her 'multicultural history', as her father was a senior diplomat, and she had spent most of her childhood and adolescence in different countries around the world. She had attended an International School whose main language was French. A few sessions after this, she informed me that she had checked my publications and found that I had published in French, so from then on, she would frequently intersperse long sections of French into her conversation with me.

My non-response to these various assertions visibly frustrated her - she sighed loudly, raised her eyes to the ceiling, and made emphatic gestures with her hands. She also complained bitterly about the 'no smoking' sign in the entrance to the building, and angrily rejected the idea that she might like to lie on the couch. She was always exquisitely made-up and heavily perfumed. She kept her coat on for the first few months of sessions, and made a frequent point of wrapping it tightly round her, and making sure that it covered as much of her legs as possible. She sat resolutely in the middle of the couch, and stared either dispassionately or scornfully at me for most of the sessions. All these procedures were clearly designed to let me know that she did not 'think much of me', that I was 'some kind of servant' who was just there to 'deal with her shit', and that she 'did not give a fuck' who I was or what I thought of her.

Nonetheless, there were deeper levels of resistance there, accompanied by powerful paranoid self-defensiveness. My remaining quiet and holding her gaze through these episodes inevitably provoked lines like... 'I know you don't like me'... but my non-response to these too eventually enabled her to relax, and (as she put it) 'think as if you are not there'. Within the third month of sessions, she started to take her coat off and lie immediately on the couch. She began to dress very seductively. On one occasion, she wore a very low-cut blouse, and, after a few minutes, interrupted the flow of her thoughts with: 'I'm wearing a wonder-bra, have you noticed?'. When I confirmed that I had noticed that she was wearing a low-cut blouse, she simply said 'Thank God!', and seemed to relax. She went on quietly to say that it was crucial for her to know that I was 'there' and 'looking' at her. She found the couch 'really scary' sometimes, because she suddenly thought 'there is nobody there'.

The more she relaxed with me, the more her thoughts became scene-orientated. She spent whole sessions going into a single scene, and increasingly appreciated my asking questions of detail about it. She also began to write up her recollections of each session in great detail, and to highlight my questions and her 'revisions' in different colours. At this point in the analysis, she became very enthusiastic about 'her work' in sessions, and declared that she had made 'enormous progress'. The 'progress' was mostly in connection with a 'scene from her marriage' (she frequently referred to films of Ingmar Bergman) which had occurred four years ago.

One scene involved waking up at night, looking at her watch and 'thinking it was afternoon', then opening the bathroom door, to find her husband standing by the toilet. She had thought that he was urinating, so went to look - hoping to find an 'erotic prospect' -, but actually discovered that her husband was masturbating. He was so shocked that he knocked down the toilet seat; she was so shocked 'by the thud of the seat' that she fainted. When she came round, she still thought it was afternoon, but looked at her watch again to see it was three in the morning. Her husband was lying on the floor beside her, distraught and in floods of tears. He confessed to her his compulsion to 'cottage' (the mutual exhibition and sometimes masturbation of genitals practised by male homosexuals in public toilets). She had not the faintest idea that he might be homosexual, but, even so, was not shocked. Rather, she felt 'dropped' into her own 'ultimate separation from everyone and everything'.

In her extensive de-translation of this scene in sessions, a surplus of erotic associations emerged from the key elaborative terms employed in various narrations. The term 'cottage' provoked thoughts of a 'retreat' her Mother had bought in Oxfordshire after inheriting money, where my patient had once spent a weekend with a Brazilian lover who was 'wonderfully endowed' - he had proudly told her that, in Portuguese, you say that very large penises 'drop down from God'. A huge divide built up at this point between this lover and her husband, whom she began to describe as 'inadequately' and then 'pathetically' endowed: in one extensive de-translation, she played with shifting the various subject-positions in the scene around the toilet, and speculated that her 'erotic prospect' at that time was 'miss-placed' (as spelt in her session notes), because her husband's erect penis 'could never get to her' if she sat on him.

As this de-translation progressed, my position in the divide became increasingly ambivalent: either she put me in a position where I could not 'get to her', or alternatively, I had 'dropped down from God'. The more she felt she was making progress, the further away she drew from her husband. Six months into the analysis, she decided to leave him, and, a day later, moved into a luxury flat in Soho. She became much more fraught about whether I was still 'looking at her'. She started phoning me up at times during the day when she thought she would get the answer phone, and would leave the message 'are you there?' In one session, she told me that she had phoned my home number, and spoken to my son, whom she was sure 'did not love me'. The next session, she apologized, burst into tears, and felt faint. When she recovered, she told me that she had started to have a recurrent fantasy - which was a 'sort of lucid dream' (she read widely in the psychology section of the local book shop): in the fantasy/lucid dream, she would choose a man she knew, who would then secretly unlock the door of her new flat, and creep in behind her. There was a crucial moment when they would either 'enter her from behind', or the whole fantasy would stop. She masturbated throughout the process, and she would only be able to achieve orgasm if the chosen fantasy man entered her. On the previous night she had chosen me to be the man in her fantasy/lucid dream, and it had not worked. I had not 'entered her from behind', and she had not achieved orgasm.

For several months after this, she was anxious and distraught in sessions. She would frequently cry throughout, and periodically hold out her hand in an angry and frustrated way to ask for tissues. She berated me for 'ruining' her fantasy/lucid dream, and accused me of 'planting the idea in her head' that she was to blame for it all - an idea produced after her recognition that she never saw, or 'got to look at', the men who secretly opened the door. The sessions became increasingly silent and emotionally charged, and she resumed a 'diss-missive' manner (her spelling in her session notes) and began to keep her coat on. Finally, she missed a session - or, at least, I believed that she had missed a session, because I waited for her. The next session, she furiously accused me of 'forgetting about her' and missing the session. She claimed to have pushed the buzzer on numerous occasions over a period of ten minutes, and received no reply. I was so perturbed by the conviction of her account that I requested a test on the door-buzzer, only to be told that it was perfectly functional. I informed her that I had requested such a test, and she seemed greatly relieved by this.

The missed session formed a central transference-stalling in the analysis. My reinforcement of her point of view - through requesting the test - was vital. It reinforced her sense of my 'looking at her', and that she was 'still in the picture'. Curiously, the main de-translative issue that emerged after the stalling concerned the 'thud' of the toilet seat. She had sudden powerful recollections of being dropped by her mother when she was a very young child (she speculated that she was between two and three). She was panic-stricken that her mother had meant to drop her, and indeed had chosen the hard scullery floor to inflict maximum damage. She still believed that she bore a scar on her forehead from the incident, and this is why she continuously wore make-up.

In this context, it would have been totally inadequate to interpret for her the fear of 'being dropped' as a main trans-ferential structure that emerged in analysis. Such an interpre-tation would miss precisely the sensory and somatoform embossing of the transferential material - notably the sense of weight, and being 'pulled' or 'sucked' downwards, which variously configured and modified her objects of desire, such as her husband and her lover's penises, her own breasts, and her faeces as a child (associated with the 'thud' of the toilet seat). Moreover, following de-translation of these varied drop-spirals of desire, the new translation - specific erotic fan-tasy - actually enabled her to form new articulations between somatoform 'sensitive' areas: the penis 'reached up' to her from 'behind', whilst she masturbated herself; she could feel safe 'with her back turned' - and not fear that her back would drop to the floor (as in the infantile scene); and she could 'know' who it was behind her, without having to check whether he was 'looking at her'. Of course, none of this 'dis-solved' the transference, nor effected productive 'knowledge' of the desire itself (such as in orgasm). It did enable her, how-ever, to shift the context in which she worked with being dropped. Rather than being 'dropped in the knowledge' - as elaborated in the 'scene from her marriage' - she was able to drop the marriage herself, which was one of her unexpressed wishes in entering analysis.

CHAPTER 6

INTERPRETATION AND CONSTRUCTION

Does it matter whether the analyst's interpretations in a session are right or wrong? How indeed would the analyst ever know, or be able to verify interpretations? In his classic text *Constructions in Analysis* (1937), Freud seems remarkably unperturbed by the question, and indeed suggests that it makes little difference. With slight irony, he approves of a famous critic's view that psychoanalytic interpretation is like tossing up a coin : 'Heads I win, tails you lose'[1] , which, Freud tells us, means '...if the patient agrees with us, then the interpretation is right; but if he contradicts us, that is only a sign of his resistance..' (SE.XXIII, p.257). Furthermore, Freud suggests that the analyst need not be unduly concerned about the accuracy or appropriateness of interpretations in general; for him, the model approach is offered by the manservant in Nestroy's play *Der Zerrissene* , who periodically nonchalantly reassures the audience that: *'Im Laufe der Begebenheiten wird alles klar werden'* (It will all become clear in the course of future developments) (ibid. p.265). In short, the analyst's interpretations should follow the apparent openendedness of the free-associative method. They should involve a certain spontaneity and rely on the seemingly arbitrary outcome of simple interactive games; and thus literally mimic the tossing up of a coin.

Of course, there is always the other side of the coin. There is always the speculation of the connections between the one side and other of any given coin. Speculation, moreover, of how the coin was formed in the first place, and how the images came to become pressed on each surface (*Prägung* - the striking of a coin - is analogically developed by both Freud and Lacan, cf. Lacan, 1988, p190). To extend the analogy to interpretation: speculation on how interpretation comes to be formed in the first place, and what specific traces of its origin

are left visible in its form. To explore this suggested dual sur-
face-dimensionality of psychoanalytic interpretation, Freud
proposed a primary distinction between interpretation and
construction.

Freud defined interpretation as the address of specific
detail raised in a session; and he defined a construction as a
broader, more general account of life experience. He developed this distinction further through an archeological
metaphor in which interpretation addresses the surface,
whereas construction comes after interpretation has excavat-
ed away considerable surface layers to expose forms of strati-
fication. Following this analogy, Freud argued that interpretation works specifically with *present* material, whereas the construction relates to the *past*. Interpretations engage the visible
evidence of unconscious process in what is represented in the
session - such as the pictographic or thing-presentation intrusion in language and dream imagery[2]; and constructions
address unconscious process in memory, and engage the long-
term structures of a given symptom or pathology.

As with much of Freud's conceptualization of clinical technique, this distinction implies a critical transparency in which
both interpretation and construction reflect, rather than provoke or enact, the real condition and the real past of the
patient. There is no engagement with the interpretation or
construction dynamics themselves, particularly with their
unconscious structuring. There is no discussion of the repression, limits, or excess produced by interpretation or construction in analysis. There is no discussion either of what might
constitute the 'success' of interpretation and construction,
other than the witty opening evocation of the coin-flipping
exercise.

The peculiar legacy of this Freudian distinction has been
provocatively developed by Laplanche. Laplanche relates
interpretation to his 'word-for-word' method of translation, in
which the analyst-translator looks first to every word, uttered

in all its thing-presentation, rather than to the syntactic unity and narrative development of the original patient-speaker (Laplanche, 'The Wall and the Arcade', in Fletcher & Stanton, 1992). Looking to the single word destroys the flow of the text, and subverts the assumed narrative closure - the 'story of my life' elements in the patient-speaker's associative outpourings. Construction for Laplanche is therefore *re-construction* ; after the destruction or de-construction of the word-for-word, there needs to be a re-construction. Central, and most controversial, in this approach, is Laplanche's allocation of interpretation to the analyst's side, and construction to the patient's side. For Laplanche, constructions are to be left exclusively to the patient [3] . This accords with his famous and frequent invocation to analysts: 'Hands off the (self) theorization of the patient' (Laplanche, 1992, p.70).

On the surface, this appears a stark, minimalist point of view. It is not difficult to imagine, for example, how an analyst's refusal, in a word-for-word way, to follow the patient's main story lines, might actually generate huge resistance, if not closure of the analysis. Laplanche's point, however, is to counter interpretative induction in the analysis - particularly the pervasive indoctrination of the patient with the analyst's theoretical orientation. In this context, it is not just the integration of the patient's narrative into set theory that is noxious, but the construction of 'interpretation' itself. Laplanche argues that the whole debate on the nature of analytic interpretation has been compromised by crude and naive assumptions: the 'realist' or 'determinist' model of interpretation aims at the recuperation of a 'real' history; and the 'creative hermeneutic' model proposes that everything is constructed, including history, so that there can be no 'raw' facts, only interpreted ones (Laplanche, 'L'interprétation entre déterminisme et hermeneutique: une nouvelle position de la question', 1993[a]). By introducing different forms of linear causality - the 'real' historical and the 'inner-world creative' causality -

each of these models of interpretation fails in its own way to address the residual irreducibility (the enigma) of the patient's discourse. If we maintain that the patient is unaware of a great part of what he says, and that analysts have inadequate or imperfect means of putting into form or theorizing what is said to them, then interpretation itself must assume a more direct and non-reductive function. Laplanche proposes therefore a direct indicative function for interpretation - such as 'talking' or 'communicating' in the sense of 'sending out a message' - rather than a hermeneutic function. Moreover, he also argues that this view is supported by the original German term - *Deuten auf* - which means to indicate with one's finger or to point out with one's eyes.

The main structural, and indeed political, point in this definition is the need to introduce an 'other' perspective into the analytic process. This 'other' perspective points to (*deuten auf*) the unconscious - the 'to be translated' (*à traduire*), all that remains unprocessed and eludes the indications/interpretations of the patient and analyst. For Laplanche, this forms an enigmatic 'outside' to the analytic communication: on one level, it consists of the input of unprocessed psychic material from outside-others - that is, the inscription of another person's unconscious in the reception of their messages (and interpretations); on another level, it is the fundamental de-centering imposed by Freud's discovery of the unconscious - namely that the ego is not central to consciousness ('Ponctuation - La revolution copernicienne inachavée' Laplanche, 1993[a], pp.iv - xxxv). In Laplanchian terms then, all interpretative and constructive work in analysis continuously progresses from Ptolemaic modes ('inner world' inwardness and self-enclosure) to Copernican ones (the otherness and outsideness of unconscious process).

A definitive theme in the Copernican impulse in contemporary psychoanalysis is research. Research starts precisely at the points where issues insinuate and insist in analysis that cannot be resolved within clinical sessions. In the clinical world, two prominent extra-mural sites have had to accommodate the demands of such research, namely clinical supervision (which has been more individual than group-based), and the 'applied psychoanalysis' sections of clinical training institutes. Neither of these sites have been considered foundational: supervision is usually seen as necessary only during the training period - and very few training institutes 'train' supervisors, or attempt research in new methods of supervision; and the 'applied' interests of training institutes are notoriously unrepresented in the training programmes themselves, so postgraduate psychoanalysts inevitably gain the impression that research needs or skills are to be regarded simply as an accessory or a hobby.

In this context, a major innovation in Lacanian and Post-Lacanian training - the *cartel* [4] - has been unfortunately been overlooked by the rest of the psychoanalytic world. For Lacan, research is not only an essential element of training (along with the clinical and teaching parts), but also integral to the life of psychoanalytic institutes and the psychoanalytic community as a whole. The cartel is a research group, usually with four participants, who meet regularly, at least one a month, to research an issue of common interest. Any senior, junior, affiliate or trainee member of the institute may join a cartel, and anyone may propose to form a cartel around an issue they find important. The issues may be well-covered ones - such as 'Oedipalization', or 'Feminism and Psychoanalysis' - or relatively unfamiliar ones such as 'Ekbom's Syndrome (delusions of parasitosis)', or 'the concept of "thrown-ness" (*Geworfenheit*) in clinical work'. Issues may specifically address technical issues arising in clinical work, or more esoteric and interdisciplinary themes.

For Lacan, the research function of the cartel is structured psychoanalytically, which implies that it is enabled specifically to address non-metabolized, transference, and translation issues. Above all, the cartel has to address analytically the out-side and otherness of the research, a function it can perform either by inviting any outside person whom the cartel decides could cast light on an issue, or by invoking the 'plus one' prin-ciple. In the latter case, the cartel can invite a senior specialist in the field - whom they nominate the 'plus one' - to whom they present a collective report on the progress of their research. The 'plus one' is supposed to occupy the position of analyst: she or he simply listens to the presentation, then afterwards writes an extensive report, specifically detailing issues that may need further research. When the cartel decides that it has completed its research - usually in a minimum of two years - it is encouraged collectively to write up an account of its work, first for other institute members, then later, if the report is publishable, for the general public.

There is no doubt that cartels provide an inimitable forum to foster psychoanalytic research. They oblige participants to work out common ground from their wide range of interests and clinical input; then, uncannily, they tend to home in on areas of unresolved, unprocessed, or unmetabolizable materi-al. The group inevitably either processes these areas Ptolomaically, by examining the effects of its group transfer-ence (including the varied intimate difficulties that emerge in research work); or it Copernicanizes these areas, either by bringing in an outsider, or the 'plus one', who, after all, is 'supposed to know'. Hopefully more will be made of this structure in future psychoanalytic training, and in the con-struction of post-training support networks.

[1] This is quoted in English in the original text.

[2] This follows Freud's 'considerations of representability' in the *Interpretation of Dreams*, in which the complexities of dream-thought unsuccessfully negotiate a 'translation' or 'trans-ference' (Freud uses the two terms of *übersetzung* and *übertragung* synonymously in this con-text) into dream-contents or thing-presentations. In this way, the 'thought' of towering over something could be 'translated' or 'transferred' in the dream in the image of a tower.

[3] This is a recent view of Laplanche. In *Problematiques IV*, he clearly conceived of con-structions also figuring on the analyst's side (p.100).

4 Lacan's choice of the term 'cartel' for research groups has intriguing associations: first, in 1920s France, there were notorious *cartel des gauches*, left-wing coalitions who appeared to agree on little accept their ability to disagree (hence bring down their own government); secondly, in French military language, it denotes an agreement for the exchange of prisoners (evoking Lacan's famous 'disc game' [Lacan, 1966, pp.197 ff.]); and finally, in classical tradition, it was the term used (in French and English) for a written challenge to duel.

CHAPTER 7

THE BEZOARIC EFFECT
WORKING WITH TRAUMATIC PROCESS

Trauma constitutes a major category in both general and psychological medicine. As a clinical speciality, it covers general accidents, major injuries, fractures, and dislocations; and, as a psychiatric and psychotherapeutic diagnostic category, it covers immediate and long-term mental disorder relating to extreme events including physical injury, violent and sexual abuse, torture, war, natural disasters like earthquakes or floods, accidents, and the witnessing of extreme situations such as accidental death or murder.

Before Pinel's new nosology, introduced during the French Revolution, the physiological and psychological aspects of trauma were mutually conceptualized through a theory of lesions, whose effects were articulated through the central nervous system (Foucault,1973, pp.176-180). After Pinel, psychological trauma were increasingly separately classified as 'neuroses', or as diseases of the nerves and mind with no necessary founding lesion.

Nonetheless, strong diagnostic and conceptual links still remain today between physical and psychological trauma. This is particularly evident in accounts of the affective response to trauma, notably in the analysis of pain (Van der Kolk, 1988; Pitman et al., 1990). It is not only hard, for example, to isolate physical from psychological pain, but also difficult, in the case of bodily injury, to separate the 'traumatic pain' provoked by the original event, from the long-term pain that follows it[1] . This is the main reason why, in contemporary terms, the interrelation between physical and psychological trauma is inevitably conceptualized as a complex and multiple process. There is both integral psychological processing of physical trauma, and physiological processing of psychologi-

cal trauma evident, particularly in somatoform disorders
(Noble, 1995).

In this context, it is somewhat surprising that much recent
research and therapeutic work on psychological trauma
appears to have generally moved away from the psychobiologic aspects of traumatic process towards mainly psychogenic and social definitions [2]. Indeed, the central diagnostic criterion of a 'stressor' is now standardly applied to assess
the form and severity of the trauma, and differentiate traumatic disorders from related anxiety disorders (such as
adjustment disorders). 'Traumatic stressors' are defined exclusively in terms of personal psychological or social response :
that is, by recognition of 'intense fear, helplessness, horror...or
in children...by disorganized or agitated behaviour', which
can be related to the witnessing or confrontation with 'events
that involved actual or threatened death or serious injury, or a
threat to the physical integrity of self or others' (*DSM4* , 1994,
pp. 427-428).

A main reason for this diagnostic shift towards the psychogenic and social aspects of trauma has undoubtedly been
the spectacular increase in international public awareness of
the extent and residual nature of specific forms of trauma,
notably trauma associated with war, accidents and natural
disasters, and those associated with the violent and sexual
abuse of children[3]. The profound and prolonged public concern about these traumatic forms has tended to proliferate
social and interpersonal conceptualizations of trauma, rather
than structural studies of the specific intrapsychic and psychobiologic processes of trauma.

Such bias is particularly apparent in elaborations of the two
recent main categories introduced into the diagnosis of trau-
ma-related mental disorders: Post-Traumatic Stress Disorder
(PTSD) and False-Memory Syndrome (FSM). The category of
PTSD, which emerged in 1980 in the original version of the
Third Edition of the *Diagnostic and Statistical Manual of Mental*

Disorders, prominently relied upon long-term research and therapeutic work with Vietnam War veterans (Kulka ed.,1990; *DSM3* ,1987). Similarly, intense public concern about the wide extent of childhood sexual abuse, and its long-term effects in later adult life, prompted various challenges to the basic assumption of the 'reality' of any given recollection of a traumatic event. It was in this context of general public debate that the new category of 'False Memory Syndrome' (FMS) was launched in 1992.

It is hardly surprising then that both these new categories of PTSD and FMS have served to draw specific attention to major weaknesses in the conceptualization and treatment of trauma. Some eminent authorities have even talked about fundamental 'diagnostic mislabelling' (Herman, 1992, pp.116-122). The main weaknesses that have emerged in criticism of PTSD and FMS are as follows: first, with PTSD, there is the increasingly highlighted inability to present an adequate account of the structural relationship between a supposed 'original' traumatic event and the perceived long-term 'post-traumatic' effects. Initially, it was assumed that subsequent 'recollections' of the original event were accurate, and that remembering in general was both automatic and critically self-regulatory. A traumatized person could not help but recall the original true picture. Central, in this view, were 'flash-backs', which were literally assumed to replicate aspects of, if not the whole original traumatic scene (cf. Eth & Pynoos, 1985, pp.8-9, & pp.175-176). More recently, the status of flashbacks has become increasingly problematic. Indeed, they are now often more frequently associated with dissociative and hallucinatory mental states, than with accurate memory recall (cf. *DSM3R* , 1987, pp.247-250 & *DSM4* ,1994, pp.424-427). *DSM4* has further stressed this dissociative and hallucinatory factor by adding a new diagnostic criteria for PTSD which emphasizes 'physiological reactivity on exposure to internal or external cues that symbolize or resemble an aspect of the traumatic event' (*DSM4*, 1994, p. 428). This shifts the main focus of traumatic process from a supposed recollection of a 'real' event towards forms of symbolic process 'cued up' around specific areas of 'physiological reactivity'. The 'reality' of trauma is thus transposed into the different register of subsequent symbolic processing of an original sensory or bodily reaction.

In contrast, FMS has exposed the extensive conceptual fracture lines underlying general application of the term 'fantasy' to traumatic experience. FMS has been through various cosmetic re-workings to promote potentially contradictory notions of the role of fantasy in traumatic process. One particular style of FMS suggests that all psychic life is so steeped in fantasy that traumatic experience can only ever be secondary to it. Some have suggested, for example, that 'real' trauma, whatever that might constitute, could only be insignificant in comparison to the 'fantastic' trauma of the inner world (a view mainly associated with Klein and Post-Kleinianism, which has lately been substantially criticized by Laplanche [Laplanche, 1992, p.220]). Alternatively, another particular presentation of FMS suggests that the fantasy-elaboration involved in the (re)experience of trauma - notably in the recall of sexual abuse - can be substantially explained in terms of *suggestion* - the analyst or therapist *suggests* a traumatic form for the analysand's fantasies which the analysand is not in a position to resist or criticize. In extremes of this formulation, the analyst, and analysis itself, is perceived to be traumatic, and to reiterate if not instigate an original trauma (Masson, 1989).

Unfortunately, such formulations of FMS are irreparably naive, narrow, and misleading. They are naive because they fail to recognize, let alone conceptualize, distinct uses of the term 'fantasy' - notably between fantasy as creative imagination, fantasy as unconscious mental process, and fantasy as hallucination; distinctions, incidentally which were crucial to early psychoanalytic debate on trauma, but have since become increasingly obscured[4] . Secondly, these FMS formulations are both narrow and misleading because they rely entirely on a crude distinction between trauma as 'reality' and trauma as 'fantasy'. There is no conception at all of trauma as 'symbolic' (as indicated in the *DSM4* account of flashback).

What is sadly missing therefore in contemporary accounts is a conceptualization of the intrapsychic structure of traumatic process which gives adequate attention to the psychobiology of trauma. Clearly, psychobiology in this context applies not simply to the reactive processes of the body to the shock of traumatic intrusion, but also to the complex and multiple inscription of trauma in which psychological and physiological aspects interconnect and indeed 'convert' (as in conversion or somatoform disorders), or 'translate' (to use Laplanchian terminology), from one to the other.

This field of work with trauma was opened up by Ferenczi, and it is only recently that the importance of his insights have been fully appreciated (Aron & Harris,1993; Stanton,1990, & 1993[a]). Ferenczi's substantive technical breakthroughs occurred not in connection with child sexual abuse, but through work with shell-shock victims during the First World War. In his work with shell-shock victims, Ferenczi managed to distinguish a number of structural features of traumatic process: first, the presence of a central and irreducible psychogenic element in the trauma - notably the hysterical anaesthesia of body zones and loss of body function - which bore a complex relationship to somatic or bodily process in so far as the brain's counter-lateral transfer was frequently either inoperative, or superseded; secondly, the predominance of autoplastic and alloplastic traumatic processes (which intruded upon the internal functioning and external agencies of the body respectively), neither of which were explicable or treatable following standard neurophysiological explanation (Ferenczi, 1926, pp.124-141); finally, the abandonment of a strategy devised to isolate a single 'traumatic event' to explain the 'shock', 'hysteria', or traumatic condition, and its replacement by a multiple inscription model in which the trauma was approached as a complex psychic and somatoform process, which incorporated elements of previous and subsequent 'events' in the psychic life of the patient (Ferenczi, 1926, pp.136-137). In this final structural feature of traumatic process, Ferenczi gave special place to the different temporal forms in which trauma was processed. Particularly important to him was the temporal form of 'afterwardsness' (Nachträglichkeit), by which he understood the complex temporal connection between (aspects of) different events in the past through which unprocessed traumatic material persistently re-emerged in different contexts for reprocessing. Hence the 'persistently present' quality of the 'past' trauma (its "afterwardsness"), and its residual reverberation, repetition, and reemergence in a fixed but complex form (as in the specific triggers of 'flashbacks' [Freud/Ferenczi, 1993, p.230; Stanton, 1990, pp. 85-90]).

Ferenczi's concern for the psychobiological aspects of trauma led him to explore the associative power of current medical terminology. Initially, he extended metaphorically a standard conception that stress and shock were somatically processed through the sphincters (usually through vomiting or diarrhoea). He proposed psychic forms of 'sphincter-processing' of trauma through the *globus hystericus* ' (lump in the throat), and the 'tic and itch' phenomenon (*Reiz* in German means 'stimulus' and 'fascination' as well as 'itch'). He argued that these psychically 'ventriloquize' through the body (*Bauchreden* in German literally means 'stomach-speech') a suppression or exaggeration of sphincter-expulsions: common ventriloquisms were constipation, diarrhoea, and ptyalism (overproduction of spit) [cf. Ferenczi, 'Ptyalism in an Oral-erotic' (1923), 2, p.315; & 'Organ Neuroses and their Treatment' (1926), 3, p.26].

Later, when working with severely traumatized, sexually

abused patients, Ferenczi used more pathogenic processes to explore psychic analogies. Crucial here was the category of the teratoma. A teratoma is a unique form of tumour which contains all three of the germ layers of the developing embryo: it has skin and nervous tissue from the ectoderm, intestinal and glandular epithelium from the endoderm, and fibrous tissue, bone and muscle from the mesoderm. Teratomae are found most commonly on the ovaries (where they usually contain hair and teeth) and testes (where they are often malignant), and less commonly on the sacrococcygeal region, anterior mediastinum, thyroid region of the neck, retroperitoneum, and the central nervous system close to the pineal body (Ashley, 1972).

Ferenczi was particularly struck by the basic structural features of the teratoma which could be metaphorically applied to trauma: first, the etymological root of the term - teratoma is the Greek word for 'monster' - had a clear literary as well as medical use, and was notably applied in contemporary literary criticism to describe fictional figures like Frankenstein and Mr. Hyde; secondly, the various forms of tissue (bone, hair etc.) coexistent in the teratoma could readily be seen as analogous to the 'unprocessed' elements of an original traumatic experience; finally, one current explanation of teratoma - which proposed the tumorous growth of an original undeveloped embryonic twin - could be extended metaphorically to suggest a double or multiple personality structure that emerged in response to trauma[5].

Undoubtedly, the teratoma remains a powerfully evocative analogy for traumatic process, and it is unfortunate that Ferenczi had no time to develop it further. It poignantly focusses on general psychobiologic failure to process violent and intrusive aspects of trauma, and the persistence of these unprocessed, unsymbolized implants as 'tumours' which may or may not become malignant, subject to future possible tumour-wall infringement (through new or 'cumulative' traumatic experience [cf.Khan,1963]). It also conveys the raw 'organic thought' or 'primary sensory imagery' often associated with traumatic experience: the teratoma's bits of unrelated hair, bone, and muscle suggest the residual fragmentary form of 'flashback' trauma scenarios in which disconnected splashes of colour, sound or smell remain evanescent, but ultimately refuse to connect associatively with a 'total picture' of an original traumatic event.

Even so, the teratoma analogy also conveys other powerful associations which seem less appropriate in the light of contemporary work with traumatic process. First of all, the teratoma is a fixed and primal embryonic structure, which is not essentially transformed through traumatic intrusion. This may well fit in with Ferenczi's theories of the ontogenetic reiteration of phylogenetic 'developmental catastrophes' , but totally fails to represent any of the complex temporal dimensions of traumatic process. Indeed, for Ferenczi, the psychic teratoma is a developmentally stuck part of the personality: '...possibly as a result of unusually profound traumas in infancy, the greater part of the personality becomes, as it were, a *teratoma* , the task of adaptation to reality being shouldered by the fragment of personality which has been spared. Such persons have actually remained almost entirely at the child level, and for them the usual methods of analytical therapy are not enough. What such neurotics need is really to be adopted and to partake for the first time in their lives of the advantage of a normal nursery' (Ferenczi, 1955,3,p.124)

The seemingly intractable problem in representing traumatic process is posed by the residual unprocessed elements of the trauma. The problem has seemed intractable because mental health professionals working with PTSD have assumed that such unprocessed elements constitute a primary irreducible inscription of the trauma. This inscription is assumed to be both pre-symbolic and fundamentally unsymbolizable. Hence the prevalence of basic sensory stimuli such as sounds and colours in clinical accounts of PTSD in children (cf.C.J. Frederick, 'Children traumatized by catastrophic situations', in Eth & Pynoos,1985,p.89). Some specialists even argue for a 'preverbal memory' of trauma, which is exclusively based on perceptual and olfactory inscriptions of an original traumatic event (L.C. Terr, 'Preverbal Memories', in Eth & Pynoos,1985, pp.65-67). Clinically, the problems and tensions arise when the specialist tries to elicit associations from these primal inscriptions, and to suggest that they represent *something* . Thematic Apperception Tests (TATs), for example, have proven spectacularly inappropriate on this level, simply because such primal inscriptions afford no thematic articulation, hence tend to be typified rather as 'abstractions' or 'autonomous fragments'. The squiggle game is equally inept here: Winnicott's 'Bob' case, for example, illustrates precisely the extent to which a therapeutic intervention aimed at forcing a child's persistent 'abstract' squiggles to represent *something*, can actually totally obscure the place of abstraction in a trauma syndrome (Winnicott, 1971, pp 64-88)[6] .

In recent years, Jean Laplanche has enabled a substantial new theorization of primary traumatic inscriptions through the concept of the 'enigmatic signifier' . The signifier - or message, as he now prefers to call it - is enigmatic in so far as it comes from the 'other'; either the other (adult) person, as in the case of child sexual abuse, or other thing (or otherness in general) in cases of violent abusive intrusion or injury. The signifier or message from the other person or thing is implanted, or intromitted in violent abusive situations; this means that it is registered in a basic sensory way, but is later accessible to some processing (or 'de- and re- translation', as Laplanche calls it). Elements of the enigmatic message are also unprocessable - notably the unconscious sexual or violent elements expressed by the other person. These elements form fixed residual structures of unprocessed material, which Laplanche calls 'psychotic enclaves'. In many ways, psychotic enclaves resemble Ferenczian 'teratomae', with the exception that Laplanche regards the enclaves as intergenerational. The unprocessed traumatic material is not only passed on from adult to child, but from generation to generation [7] This explains the long-term historical persistence of traumatic effects; why, for example, later generations of holocaust survivors or indeed of concentration camp attendants, reproduce specific features of PTSD.

*

It is commonly argued that there is a primacy of the image over verbal elaboration in the psychic processing of trauma. This is not to say that verbal accounts of trauma are dislocated from the visual, but that they are secondary and *elaborative* In therapy, much of the work on trauma issues from elaboration of images - or series of images, or *scenes* - and the traumatic form is further configurated (often enigmatically) in the verbal account. Verbal accounts can further encrypt salient image features of the trauma, notably as unconscious defence against further psychic wounding and pain[8]. Although there has been a general recognition of the complexity of the relationship between visual and verbal elaboration of trauma - in which visual and verbal elements remain essentially separate - little consideration has been given to the integrative process of visual and verbal material in traumatic experience. This 'integration' is usually either assumed to be entirely unconscious (that is, 'visible' only through the effects of displacement and condensation in later accounts of trauma); or assumed to be absent, so that trauma becomes characterized as entirely 'de-integrated' (that is, as articulating a primal irreversible dislocation between visual and verbal elements, or 'psychotic fragmentation' [bizarre thoughts] following current classification).

An alternative approach is to view the integrative process of visual and verbal elements in trauma as *translative* (cf. Jean Laplanche, 'Traumatisme, Traduction, Transfert et autres

Trans(es)', in Laplanche,1993[a]). As with a translation from one language to another, psychic processing of traumatic experience involves the continuous recasting of visual material in verbal form. Like all translations between languages, the new version misses whole areas of the original. In verbal translation of visual elements of traumatic experience, some important and indeed primal elements remain untranslated. They remain 'stuck' and unprocessed in verbal narratives, and intrude into, or disrupt the standard linearity of narrative process. As these unprocessed visual elements remain unsymbolized, they have no ready referent and do not resemble or refer to 'objects' in the symbolized narratable world. They appear to encapsulate and intensify therefore primary visual elements such as colour (or sometimes black and white), or abstract form. Abstraction articulates the unprocessed visual elements of traumatic experience, and indeed both encapsulates and focuses psychic pain[9] (Stanton, 1993[b]).

What emerges then in the progressive attempts of traumatized people to represent or 'narrate' their trauma, and forge some direct contact with their pain, is a form of *psychic contusion* (Stanton, 1995). As with a physical contusion, where a blow from the outside of the body provokes various forms of internal disruption including progressive blood coagulation, psychic contusion develops a similar reactive process of disruption, blockage and coagulation. Like the spread of a bruise, the internal translative process is visible from the outside by the intensification and shift of colour. The process is articulated through blocks of coagulated traumatic material - or *contundors* - which shift and intensify like the colours of a bruise. Contundors [10] carry the primary impact of the trauma and coagulate primal sensory (visual and auditory) material. As with bruises, contundors convey the most sensitive psychic spots: they are prime articulation points between the inner and outer worlds, so trigger traumatic associations; they grow and diminish associatively through the processes of symbolization and working through; and they can be cumulative, as repeated trauma, such as violent or sexual abuse, so deepen the bruise and adjoin further contundors (Khan, 1963).

Like Bion's beta-elements (Bion, 1984), or Laplanche's 'source-objects' (Laplanche, 1993[a]), contundors resist and disrupt symbolic elaboration (or 'linking'). Their difference from beta-elements and source-objects lies in their violent intrusive origin, which forecloses subsequent symbolization and 'normal thought process'. In this context, Laplanche has indeed recently suggested that there is a fundamental difference between traumatic and other forms of psychic process (Laplanche, 'Implantation, Intromission', in Laplanche, 1993[a]), but he has not yet begun to elaborate on the knock-on effect this might have on other distinctions, such as those between neurotic and psychotic, homogenous and exogenic psychic processes.

In the psychotherapeutic context, contundors emerge as the sensitive spots of the psychic contusion. Often, from the outset, traumatized people set broad boundaries for their trauma, and give some account of their traumatic experience, though, of course, there is the common incidence of immediate or delayed amnesia and foreclosure. What is difficult for both the traumatized person and the analyst is to relate to, and represent *the specific contusive process itself* , because this involves sensitivity to the shifts and failures of narrative in the repeated replay in analysis of traumatic material. To extend the analogy: this is like running your fingers repeatedly over a bruise to locate the various levels and points of pain. In therapy, the main painful points - the contundors - are likely to emerge through transference-stallings, when initially there is pain but no significant image or associative production, and the patient loses touch with the analyst (or vice versa in countertransference). Contundors are images or sounds that carry intense pain (and often anxiety), which may or may not carry verbal associations (which will inevitably relate to secondary attempts to 'translate' the trauma). Contundors are usually experienced as 'abstract', 'other', inexplicable, intrusive and threatening. They can be - or be seen to be - hallucinatory, and intensify or condense the coagulatory effect of primary visual and auditory elements at the expense of 'representation'. In short, colour, or lack of colour (black and white), or dissonance, threaten to break down the iconic order and the referential sense of a visual or auditory world: objects 'out there' break down into pure colour or absence of colour, and language breaks down into disordered or amplified sound.

The emergence or intrusion of contundors in therapy is therefore difficult, if not impossible, to process. To enable any translative process whatsoever to occur, the analyst has to recognize and stay with the contundor, and not interpret it away for the patient, or suggest that it is 'all right' - part of a 'normal' response to trauma - which, in the experience of the patient, it clearly is not[11].

What is possible - and often productive - is to stay with the contusive effect of the contundor. One patient of mine, a German woman in her late 50s, was referred to me for treatment for severe panic attacks. These seemed totally arbitrary to her, though she had been violently and sexually abused by her father during her childhood. Nonetheless, the arbitrary feeling about these attacks only served to heighten their future potential threatening and overwhelming nature: 'time-bombs' she called them! In her case, the contusive effect - which we stayed with for four sessions after the first panic attack experienced during the time she was in analysis - was of the ground 'giving way' under her feet. The main associative material that this brought up for her was of her father's body 'giving way'. He had died quickly, but in great pain, of cancer of the kidneys, and she had personally looked after him during his last months, as her mother was obliged to continue work to support the family. My patient was in her early teens at this time.

Although it became increasingly clear that she had not been able to mourn and work through important aspects of her father's death, there was still no indication of how this related to the circumstances of her panic attacks. This was a source of great frustration for her - and indeed led her to think that the connection with her father's death was some magical induction of mine - even though she felt that the connection had put her on 'more solid ground'.

A few weeks later, she experienced a further panic attack. This time, she was clearly aware of the circumstances which had provoked it. She had been playing with her 6 year old granddaughter in the park, and had trodden on the soft rubber material that is placed beneath childrens' swings. She had felt 'the ground give way', and had an overwhelming impression of the colour red all around her. In subsequent sessions main features of the contundor began to emerge: soft material - she recalled a previous attack provoked on holiday by pushing a cigarette into a tin ashtray; and the colour red, which was always there, and was strongly associated with blood - and here she recalled another attack provoked by inadvertently standing on a beetle, and lots of red blood squirted out.

At this point in the analysis, she felt enabled to process the complexity of these two main features of the contundor. She suddenly recalled finding bits of soft red metal around the house as a child. They had always puzzled her. She then remembered her father explaining to her during his last months that this metal was an essential part of a bomb-triggering mechanism which had radically improved the effectiveness of German incendiary bombs just before the start of the Second World War. He had been a very minor member of the large research team that produced this metal, but nonetheless felt deeply guilty and responsible for the destruction of British cities, particularly Coventry, during the war. Indeed he was convinced that his final illness was God's punishment for this, and he repeatedly told her this during his last months. This thought had terrified her then, and still terrified her when it emerged with great difficulty in the session. She was profoundly shocked by the depth of her horror of it, and her intense resistance to it.

Finally, the colour red recalled for her the blood that her father urinated during the last weeks of his life. She had to help him up to the toilet, and flush it away. She was terrified that his body was 'giving way', and that he was literally pissing out all his insides.

Obviously, there are many further issues involved in this example, notably those relating to the trans-generational transmission of trauma, the trans-traumatic links with the earlier violent and sexual abuse, and the whole issue of cumulative traumatic process. Nonetheless, the main point I wish to illustrate here is the connection in analysis between work on the contusive effect and the emergence of the contundor. I have given more detailed examples of this elsewhere, with specific reference to the transference dynamics involved (Stanton, 1994[b]).

*

Everyone directly involved with traumatic experience is aware of the importance and persistence of repetition in that experience. This repetition is complex and indeed multi-layered. There is the involuntary repetition of auditory and visual material relating to the trauma, or 'flashbacks' (a notion we criticized earlier); then there is the repetition of obsessional or delusional thoughts relating to the trauma, including, sometimes, in abusive traumatic situations, fixed identifications with the aggressor; finally, there is the repetition of the experience of 'overview' of the trauma, when the traumatized person feels they can separate from previously intrusive and overwhelming traumatic material and provide a working account of the trauma. This process is very evident - if not highlighted - in analytical work with trauma. The corollary experience of dissolution of these periods of overview - and indeed of the succession of periods of different overview - are equally highlighted in analytical work.

Repetition, in each of these forms, does not amount to the return to something static and fixed, but a dynamic process in which the various elements of traumatic experience are successively re-translated. To return to the contusion analogy: the colours of the bruise shift along with the internal process of coagulation, fragmentation, and partial reintegration. The experience of repetition, and of the fundamental rootedness of the trauma, is generated by the contundors - by the focal points of pain as the metaphorical fingers re-run across the bruise. But these points themselves enlarge, diminish, and relocate. A prime task of analytical work with trauma is therefore to come to terms with this repetitive shift of contundors in the psychic reprocessing of traumatic experience.

To explore further this repetitive shift of contundors, I would like to introduce the concept of the *bezoaric effect*. The bezoaric effect can be defined as the repetitive re-presentation of contundors in traumatic process. The operative analogy here is with the production of the bezoar stone, which is a calculus or digestory ball produced by camels, antelopes and deer that have to survive in difficult mountainous or desert terrain. Such animals periodically cough up a ball of undigested food, which they then repeatedly swallow again for further nutritive processing. When the ball can provide no more nutrition, the animal finally discards it. At this stage, the ball has become solid and stone-like, and contains interwoven strands of different materials such as grass, bark, flowers, sand, and insect shell. Such stones are delicately and sometimes brightly coloured, and are highly treasured as works of art by nomadic tribes in the Middle East (particularly in Persia).

The production dynamics of a bezoar stone poignantly evoke structural aspects of the psychic process of traumatic experience. In analysis, the ball of undigested or 'untranslated' material is periodically 'coughed up', affording the periods of overview described earlier, where the focal points of pain (the contundors) become temporarily fixed and visible. With repeated coughings-up, the shifts of constituency and arrangement of undigested material also become temporarily fixed and visible. At some point then - to extend fully the analogy - the structure of contundors solidifies, and the material is not further internalized for reprocessing. At this point - which we might provocatively call the 'end' of an analysis[12] - the bezoar stone, with its raw untranslatable contundors, becomes like a work of art. The traumatized person becomes ultimately familiar with the ley-lines and spots of pain, but can also contemplate the whole stone, appreciate its form, and even its peculiar beauty. This may help explain the special way in which traumatized people come to value and even treasure what they have experienced from their trauma.

*

The study of trauma and traumatic process has been restricted by uncritical use of outmoded conceptions of time and psychic process (See Chapter 5 above). Focus on 'post' traumatic process, in particular, has reinforced the false conception that there is a separate traumatic event in the past followed by a subsequent 'post-traumatic' syndrome. This has helped form a pervasive therapeutic orientation towards capturing the traumatic past, rendering it conscious, thus supposedly amenable to control. In contrast, we have argued here for a conception of trauma as an ongoing translative process, in which the original sensory traumatic impression is continuously re-presented through contundors - primary complex and unprocessed traumatic signifiers. The traumatized person's attempts to 'translate' contundors provokes shifts in the complex structure of their traumatic experience, variously highlighting the untranslatable or unprocessable elements in that experience. The ongoing translative process itself therefore articulates its own periodic 'coughings-up' of untranslated traumatic experience - or the bezoaric effect of trauma.

The new concepts of psychic contusion, contundor, and bezoaric effect introduced here relate to problems generated within psychoanalytic approaches to trauma since Ferenczi. Obviously these concepts will have to establish their use-value, and convince mental health professionals not always favourably predisposed towards psychoanalytic approaches.

[1] Research on PTSD in Israeli soldiers following the Lebanon War indicated that the pain of injuries was often perceived as more 'traumatic' than the actual event itself. There is a detailed study, for example, of a soldier who lost an eye in battle, for whom the extreme pain following the incident (when he was left untreated) compacted the treatment of PTSD symptoms (See Chapter 5, Note 1)

[2] This trend should be contrasted with a small but significant development of PTSD using biological models, notably to study alterations in hypothalamic-pituitary-adrenal axis functioning, as well as serotonergic, noradrenergic, and optoid changes.

[3] PTSD after accidents has recently attracted considerable public attention, notably in the context of legal disputes over substantial insurance claims by PTSD sufferers. Particularly interesting here has been the controversial, and now largely discredited, opinion, that only 'real' observation of severe accidents or death to someone very dear can provoke PTSD; in which case, the observation of the death of someone dear on the television would supposedly be 'unreal' and produce a different effect (cf. Aisling Campbell, 1995).

[4] Jung first introduced the distinction between *Phantasieren* (creative imagination), *Phantasie* (unconscious fantasy), and *Phantasma* (hallucination) into the debate on complex formation in trauma (Jung, 'The Theory of Psychoanalysis', 1961).

[5] It should also be noted that some research does indicate a significant psychogenic factor in teratomic development (Chipkevitch & Fernandes, 1993).

[6] One reading of this could be *'s countertransferential resistance to the evident psychotic processes involved (implicit in his own evocation of 'schizophrenia' [Winnicott, 1971, p.70]; cf. Stanton, 1994a).

[7] Laplanche sets this in the context of Freud's discussion of 'taboos' (Fletcher & Stanton, 1992, pp.35-36).

[8] Nicholas Abraham and Maria Torok strikingly illustrate the scope and potential of such encryptment in their analysis of the Russian language cryptonomy in the Wolf Man Case History (Abraham & Torok, 1986).

[9] Sound should also be mentioned in this context: dissonance frequently figures in accounts of traumatic experience. This whole field - and its implicit appeal to separate orders of primal sound and symbolized sound (music) - is yet to be explored (Dunn, 1996).

[10] To 'contund' in old English means to beat from the outside. The term 'contundors' is

introduced here to name the psychic material that carries out the process of contusion.

11 The primary asymmetry of the situation - that the analyst cannot have any experience or 'idea' of the patient's trauma -constantly threatens to foreclose clinical work. This is particularly the case with group trauma in combat and accident-related contexts - where the analyst is constantly open to questions like 'how could you ever know what it is like to be under fire? or in a plane that crashes?' and so forth. There are informed arguments here that group work with such trauma-survivors is initially more appropriate, and that individual psychotherapy can later address long-term issues in depth.

12 By this, I also mean the end of self-analysis, and not just the end of formal analytic sessions.

CHAPTER 8

AFTERWARDSNESS
THE PROBLEM OF TIME

Contemporary psychoanalysis, like contemporary psychiatry and clinical psychology, generally still employs late 19th century conceptions of temporality in relation to both psychic process and disorder. It relies almost exclusively on the assumption of a linear progression of 'real' events, which can either be consciously accessed through memory, or can unconsciously intrude in psychic life in the form of 'flashbacks', which are usually prompted by real traumatic events in the past. Even when fantasy is primarily involved, and it is assumed, for example, that an abusive event is fantasized rather than 'real', it is equally assumed that the form of the fantasy still has a 'real' basis in an interpersonal, collective, or even genetically inherited past. A linear progression is still there, though it is extended interpersonally through identification, projection and introjection; and extended generationally through an assumed collective historical past.

Such assumptions ignore major contemporary developments in the conception of temporality. First and foremost, they miss radical research into the nature of temporalization (*Zeitlichkeit*), that is, the form of psychic production of time[1] . The most important developments here have occurred within the sphere of experiential, or existential time. In this sphere, Bergson initially influenced the dynamic orientation of research, through focussing on the *élan* and *flux* of time[2]. He pioneered specific concern for the narrative qualities of time - the 'befores' and 'afters' of stories derived from the present tense, and the relative 'timelessness' of disordered narratives produced by an *abaissement du niveau mental*[3] . Later, Heidegger explored other modes of temporalization through the concept of *Dasein* (being-there) and its aim-orientations - such as, 'being-a-whole' (*Ganzsein*), 'being-towards-death'

(*Sein zu Tode*), 'being-the-basis' (*Grundsein*), 'being-already' (*Schon-sein*), 'being-for-one-another' (*Für-einandersein*), etc. (Heidegger, 1967).

In this context, the location of either Freud or Jung's work on temporalization in terms of contemporary research, remains problematic. On the one hand, they both seem committed to a 'real' chronology of 'events' and 'stages' in life; and, on the other hand, they invent respectively the revolutionary new experiential time concepts of *Nachträglichkeit* (afterwardsness) and *Zurückphantasieren* (retrospective fantasy). In a crucial and formative way - as an intimate of both Bergsonian and Heideggerian approaches - openly explored reasons for frustration with this apparent contradiction: 'Freud demands a total objectivation of proof so long as it is a question of dating the primal scene, but he no more than presupposes all the re-subjectivations of the event that seem to him to be necessary to explain its effects at each turning-point where the subject restructures himself - that is, as many restructurings of the event as take place, as he puts it, *nachträglich* , afterwards. What is more, with an audacity bordering on off-handedness, he asserts that he holds it legitimate in the analysis of processes to elide the time intervals in which the event remains latent in the subject. That is to say, he annuls the *times for understanding* (le *temps* pour comprendre) in favour of the *moments of concluding* (le *moment* de conclure) which precipitate the meditation of the subject towards deciding the meaning to attach to the original event' (Lacan, 1977, p.48) [4].

This privileged focus on the re-subjectivation and temporal re-structuring of 'events' suggests that the process of temporalization itself is complex - and that *Nachträglichkeit* itself enacts a selective revision (following basic considerations of representability [5]), in which significant 'afterwards' elements are lost, removed, re-worked, and re-found.

The very complexity of this notion of a 'shifting temporal

directional form' (afterwardsness), that continuously attempts to process residual unprocessed and unconscious material by moving existentially-temporally between different directions (being-towards-wholeness, being-towards-death, etc.), has provoked strong calls for a return to simple linear chronological 'truths' within the traditional psychoanalytic community. Helmut Thomä and Neil Cheshire, for example, have recently published an extensive critique of what they call the 'French solution' to the problem of temporalization of psychic life (Thomä & <$iCheshire>, 1991). The main trend of their argument is that Freud's notion of *Nachträglichkeit* (afterwardsness) is not as complex as the French (notably Lacan, and later Laplanche) have argued. They assert that 'afterwardsness' effects have one temporal direction, hence betray a mono-causality; that is, there is a single event in the past which is repressed by the subject, and then *afterwards* is reactivated by something in the present. In short, they advocate that afterwardsness should be seen as a psychic time bomb facility with a single triggering mechanism which may be activated by fact or fantasy.

This view not only distorts Freud - notably textually in limiting and standardizing Freud's use of the term, and by exclusively privileging his use of it - but also fails to explore in depth Lacanian and Laplanchian reasons for rendering the term complex. This is particularly the case with Laplanche's dual temporal direction of afterwardsness from past to present, and then from present to past, which they simply dismiss as 'non-Freudian' (Thomä & Cheshire, 1991, p.413). This is a strange dismissal, as Laplanche takes great care to stress that his notion of 'afterwardsness' is different from Freud's, and indeed stems from a critique of the Freudian notion (cf.Laplanche, 'Notes on Afterwardsness', in Fletcher & Stanton [eds], 1992).

This difference is well illustrated by an example of Freud's use of the term that interestingly is not included in Thomä and Cheshire's 'exhaustive' list, namely in the 'Dumpling' or *Knödel* dream in the *Interpretation of Dreams* (Freud, S.E.IV, pp. 204-205). Amongst other things, this dream involves the hostess of an inn making dumplings. Freud reflects that love and hunger meet at a woman's breast, and proceeds to recount the story of a young man, who looks at a buxom wet-nurse who had once suckled him as a baby, and comments that 'I'm sorry that I did not make a better use of my opportunity' (ibid., p.204)[6] . Laplanche extracts two seemingly incontrovertible insights from this example: first that it illustrates that Freud envisioned a present-to-past orientation to afterwardsness, in the light of the young man's present re-activation of infantile drives; secondly - and ultimately more importantly - it reveals the missing factor in Freud's own theory of afterwardsness, namely the unconscious erotic input of the wet-nurse into the scene. For Laplanche, it is the implantation of the wet-nurse's unconscious sexual message that primes the young man's process of afterwardsness. It is the otherness - the enigmatic nature - of this message that structures this afterwards-situation, and gives it primacy as a temporal form. The enigmatic nature of this implanted message insists that it be processed or translated, but, of course, it is the very otherness - the unconscious sexual element - that resists translation.

*

If we focus our interpretation of clinical material on complex temporal structures, rather than on establishing linear progressions of events, then new critical priorities emerge within sessions. First of all, afterwardsness-effects haunt the time structure of sessions themselves. It becomes obvious that the various re-presentations of material follow their own complex temporal structure, which to some extent vitiate the linear containment of the fixed 50 minute session: an afterwardsness-connection (say with a detail of a previous dream) may install itself at the very end of a session, enforcing the analyst formally to close the important associative process (at least within the context of the session). Similarly, the influx of untranslated material in an afterwardsness-effect can stall a session. The patient or the analyst can feel overloaded by a sudden connection linking afterwards-elements from previously unforeseen 'scenes', and the analysis inevitably stalls here, whenever it happens to fall within the session. Jung inspirationally named this phenomenon 'reaction-time' (*Reaktionszeit*) - though his insights here have remained curiously unexplored [7] (Jung, 1905).

These dislocating effects render analytical time itself profoundly problematic. Lacan controversially proposed to address this issue by introducing the notion of a 'variable session', by which he meant that an analyst could vary the length of a session to accommodate various afterwardsness effects: it could be closed, if necessary, after an early stalling, or extended if a rich associative vein emerged late on in a session (Lacan, 1966 ,p.310). This strategy was not originally designed to be used in every session, but simply when indicated by the specific dynamics of a session; it only later became wrongly conflated with a general concept of the 'short session' - the subject of much controversy (Roudinesco, 1993, p.271).

In this context, it is easy to become totally absorbed by the important practical issues posed by such a clinical strategy, and to lose the underlying issue of how to work with the specific temporal structure of the symptom. It is obvious that the removal of a fixed timescale for sessions, and the suggestion that sessions necessarily must be 'short', introduce a powerful element of uncertainty and unpredictability into the analytical process: not least that the patient cannot know how long the session will last, and must constantly fear being cut off, both of which might produce cruel, dangerous and destabilizing effects. But excessive parody of the Lacanian short session also obscures the 'variable' option, in which 'classical' termination of a session after 50 minutes might be equally cruel, dangerous, and destabilizing, especially if the patient is in the process of working through crucial or traumatic material.

On the practical level, both of these options seem unnecessarily extreme and rigid. There is no substantive reason prohibiting an analyst from both adopting the frame of regular fixed-time sessions, and also working when appropriate with flexible options - particularly in extending the session where this might offer *necessary* containment of distress and anxiety (of not being heard out). The only difficulty with this option is that the analyst must schedule significant breaks between sessions to allow for such flexibility.

*

Freud's observation that primal image-forms (*DasBildliche*) in dreams do not readily fit into a word-frame (*Wortfassung*) (Freud, 1972, p.335), identifies a rich site to begin to explore the complex temporalization of symptoms. A primal image-form is pictorial or auditory, and is more or less translated into an object - so it could be a particular colour, or a car, or hedgehog - though its primal nature is indicated by the dislocations provoked by the words associated with it. It is primal precisely because it cannot be contained within a word-frame. Primal image-forms do not suddenly appear in sessions, but emerge through repeated representations and re-workings of images; they insinuate themselves across different narratives - particularly the dream narratives; and they become manifest through their ability to collapse or blur distinctions between previously separate events or scenes. The persistent sameness of the colour, car or hedgehog, for example, in numerous scenes collapses contextual difference between their various presentations, and therefore also undermines the affective and temporal distinction. It is possible therefore progressively to map out complex temporal structures as they emerge around the dislocations provoked by primal images in sessions.

*

A bulimic woman of 34 was referred to me because she suffered from severe depression[8]. She periodically developed paranoid thoughts that she was about to be attacked and/or raped by some unknown figure in the background. As the analysis progressed, the following important formative scenes emerged: first, during her early childhood, her parents used to fight violently at night when she, her brother and two sisters were in bed, and supposed to be asleep. One night, when she was 11, she came downstairs with her brother (who was 16) to see what was happening. They found their parents locked in bitter struggle. Her mother's face was bruised, some teeth were knocked out, and her mouth was bleeding. The brother attempted to separate them, and the father pinned him on the floor, punched him hard in the face, and repeatedly threatened to 'cut off his balls'. My patient then 'froze', and felt guilty at not being able to help him. Not surprisingly, the brother subsequently became very withdrawn from the family, and was particularly abstemious about being seen in any form of undress - 'neither in his pyjamas, nor in his swimming trunks'. She continued to feel very sorry for him, but was unable to get close to him, or to help him.

The second scene

When she was 15, her mother developed a cancerous growth on her left knee. This was surgically removed, leaving a large hole. Some sixth months later, shortly before her mother died, my patient had visited her in hospital, and was shocked to discover - when she was straightening the sheets -

that her mother's pubic hair had been completely shaved off.

The third scene

Nine years later, she had started an affair with an older man (20 years her senior). A few months into the affair, he had physically forced her to have anal intercourse with him, after which he entered her vaginally. This had terrified her, and 'permanently made her afraid of men'. The next month, she became pregnant by this man, and decided immediately to have an abortion and end her relationship to him. Prior to the abortion, the nurses shaved off her pubic hair. This horrified her and induced her to suspect that she might have cancer.

The fourth scene

At the beginning of a session about two years into the analysis, she told me she was considering ending the analysis, and set out a series of drawings of a female nude on the consulting room floor. I asked her if the drawings were of herself, and she said 'no' - they were of no one in particular. These drawings were marked by emphatic circles, which were located at different parts of the nude's body in each of the drawings (see figures 1 - 4). When asked to comment on them, she remained silent for a long time, began to cry, and then to sob deeply. She told me that she had suddenly remembered her cat, who had died unexpectedly three years ago (but this was the first time that she had mentioned the incident). The cat had developed a fierce cough, which she had put down to 'fur balls', but was later diagnosed as lung cancer. She had to have the cat put down.

---

[1] The term 'temporalization' does not easily assimilate into everyday English usage, not least because of an easily associated sense of 'temporarily', indicating the transient and ephemeral. 'Temporalization' here means a specific structural form of time - as in the temporal form in which a symptom is (re)produced.

[2] Bergsonism first entered psychoanalytic debate through Pierre Janet (who was

Bergson's student) and Jung (who was Janet's student). In the 1930s, Eugène Minkowski extensively developed Bergsonian concepts in relation to psychoanalysis, notably in his classic *Le Temps vécu* (Minkowski, 1936) - a formative text for the early Lacan.

3 This means a 'lowering of mental level', which, in Bergsonian terms, indicates a weakening of the productive and synthetic powers of the present psychic impulse (the *élan*). It is curious that this term survived, untranslated, in the mature work of Jung.

4 The terms 'the time to understand' and the 'moment to conclude' relate to Lacan's concept of 'logical time' (Lacan, 1966, 'Le temps logique et l'assertion de certitude anticipée: un nouveau sophisme'. pp.197-213; cf. Forrester, 'Dead on Time', 1990, pp.168-218).

5 This follows Freud's conception of the four modes of distortion (*Entstellung*): condensation. displacement, considerations of representability, and secondary elaboration (cf. J.F. Lyotard, 'The Dream Work Does Not Think', in *The Lyotard Reader*, ed. A. Benjamin 1993).

6 It is interesting here that Strachey transforms this reference into the past tense, and adds a footnote to suggest that the concept of 'afterwardsness' is outmoded. In fact, Freud uses the present tense: 'Ich pflege mich der Anekdote...'.

7 'Reaction-time' for Jung was initially the time that a patient took to provide an association for a word in the Word-Association Test. In the preliminary stages of his elaboration of the test, he argued simply that the longer it took to associate, the more unprocessed and complex the underlying psychic material. Later on, he developed the notion of 'reaction-time' into a complex temporal structure in its own right - in short, into the temporal articulation of the complex itself (cf Stanton, 1994c).

8 This is a case I have discussed at length in a different context (Stanton, 1994b).

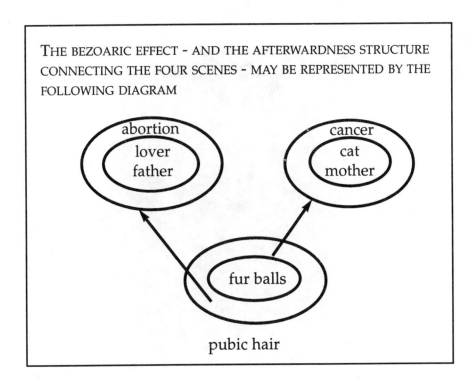

THE BEZOARIC EFFECT - AND THE AFTERWARDNESS STRUCTURE CONNECTING THE FOUR SCENES - MAY BE REPRESENTED BY THE FOLLOWING DIAGRAM

abortion
lover
father

cancer
cat
mother

fur balls

pubic hair

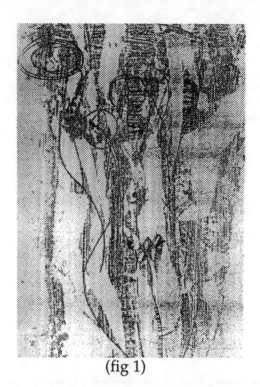

(fig 1)

(fig 2)

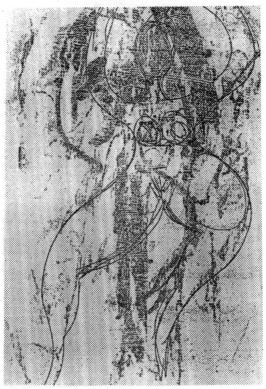

(fig 3)

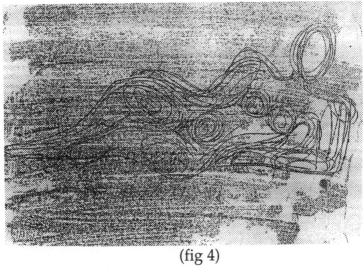

(fig 4)

CHAPTER 9

ZIPS:
THE PLACE OF SUBLIMATION
AND THE SUBLIME IN ANALYSIS

If we were to compare generally the main themes in psychoanalytic trainings in the 1930s, 40s, and 50s, with those of
contemporary trainings, an outstanding difference would be
respect for the process of sublimation. For Freud, sublimation
remained a central way in which 'culture' (*der Kultur* could
process its 'dis-ease' (*das Unbehagen*), so the sublimation
process had to be integral to both individual psychic development and the progress of individual analysis[1]. This was reinforced in various ways by Freud's immediate successors:
Melanie Klein assimilated the process of reparation
(*Wiedergutmachung*) into 'the capacity for sublimation' (Klein,
1975, 1, p206) [2]; Anna Freud privileged sublimation as a positive form of defence mechanism 'by which the ego achieves
its purpose of diverting the instinctual impulses from their
purely sexual goal to aims which society holds to be higher'
(Anna Freud, 1946, p.192); and Fenichel characterized sublimation as a 'successful' defence against 'pre-genital strivings'
which allowed and made possible 'the capacity for genital
orgasm'; whereas 'pathogenic' defences led to a whole range
of regressive perversions including homosexuality, sado-
masochism, and fetishism (Fenichel, 1946, p.141ff.).

For Freud, and his first and second generation followers,
the promotion of the patient's capacity to sublimate was
regarded as essential to psychoanalytic 'cure', with all the
social implications which this notion carried - such as
'healthy' psycho-sexual life, community spirit (*Gemeinschaft*),
and non-violent cooperative behaviour. The defining charac-
teristic of sublimation as an individual psychic process was
integration into the cohesive structures of society: the family

(through successful negotiation of the Oedipus Complex), and educational culture (*Bildung*), which demanded the acquisition of specific artistic and intellectual skills and sensitivity [3]. An important part of analysis, therefore, was both the de-sexualization of pre-genital drives, and the promotion of cultural awareness and sensitivity. It was common practice to advise a patient to read a book, or go to an opera or an exhibition. The promotion of sublimation also attested to the social responsibility and commitment of the analyst: its promotion seemed an overt way of countering regression towards socially violent and abusive behaviour, which, of course, loomed ominously between two World Wars. It is striking, in this context, that Freud believed that the crucial impetus that led people to reject violence and war was *aesthetic*: for him, it was only when pictures were released of leafless and burnt trees on First World War battlefields that serious anti-war arguments started to take root (Freud, 'Why War?'(1933), SE.XXII p.215).

If the theme of sublimation figures at all in contemporary psychoanalytic training programmes, it is simply as a minor element of Freudian metapsychology. There is certainly no 'curative' aim attached to it, and no social imperative. Psychoanalysts are not encouraged to promote sublimation, unless the term is (erroneously) read as a derivative of reparation or successful ego-functioning. There are many reasons for this: first, with the help of Bion, Foulkes, and others, we are now aware that the group psychic process cannot simply be reduced to forms of individual and family psychic process, so wars and general violent behaviour cannot necessarily be contained and controlled within the parameters of individual analysis (Bion, 1961, pp.187-190); secondly, the notions of a 'normal' or 'genital' (hetero) sexuality, governed exclusively by successful (positive) or regressive (negative) individual negotiations of the Oedipus Complex, have been powerfully and effectively criticized - even though a small orthodox minority hold these notions dear [4]; finally, the associated notions of 'health' (including 'social health') and 'cure', have become theoretically and practically problematic, which has led to general policies of prophylaxis rather than support for ultimate life-aims (such as are encapsulated in the term 'cultural education' [*Bildung*]).

Nonetheless, it is still curious that the vast majority of psychoanalytically-orientated clinicians today discard sublimation as obsolete in contemporary clinical practice. The notable exception to this trend is Jean Laplanche. In his third volume of the *Problematiques, La Sublimation (Laplanche,1980)*, he exhaustively examines the tensions and ambivalences in Freud's conceptualization of the sublimation process, and arrives at two residual areas of interest: the sublime in its philosophical context (from Burke and Kant to Lyotard and Derrida); and the sublime as chemical analogy - sublimation as the direct transformation of a substance from solid to gas without passing through a liquid stage - which Laplanche reads analogically to cast light on the process of de-sexualization of the drives (Laplanche, 1980, pp.18-19).

What have these two areas - the philosophical sublime and chemical sublimation - to offer to contemporary clinical work? Let us turn, first of all, to the philosophical sublime. Here the notion carries two distinct evocations: first, there is the *descriptive* sublime, which denotes vast and powerful objects and experiences; and then an *evaluative* sublime, which traditionally relates to exceptional works of art (cf. Crowther, 1989, p.2ff.). Freud is fully aware of this tradition, but clearly fails to distinguish these evocations: in his study of Leonardo, for example, the evaluative sublime of the *Giaconda's* smile is rendered unproblematically into the terms of the descriptive sublime of the young Leonardo's infantile * fantasies (Freud, S.E.XI, pp.86). This has dramatic and unsuspected effects: on the one hand, it suggests that the evaluative sublime - or great art - is present within the sublimation process of all of us, and so, by extension, analysts should look for, respect and foster this artistic sublime in the work of their patients in sessions; and, on the other hand, it suggests the ultimate primacy of the descriptive over the evaluative sublime, which implies a founding pathology of the sublime. It is interesting that post-Freudian analysts have tended to focus exclusively on the latter effect, at the expense of the former. Fenichel, for example, claimed that: 'Just as with certain identifications, sublimations too, may more or less successfully combat and undo infantile destructive impulses, but also and in a distortive fashion give way to these same destructive impulses; in a certain sense, every artistic fixation on a natural process is a "killing" of this process' (Fenichel,1946, p.142).

For Laplanche, the chemical analogy for the sublimation process emphatically counteracts such a narrow reading, and suggests rather a transformation of a substance from a primary physical state to a tertiary one, without any intermediate stage. In this context, sublimation is not a "killing" of a natural process, but a specific transcendence of it in the classical sense of the word (i.e. 'the conveyance of a drawing or a design from one surface to another, especially to a lithographic stone '*Oxford English Dictionary*, 1839). Sublimation both 'jumps' the liquid stage, and infringes the natural 'assumption' of an axial progression from solid to liquid to gas.

The chemical analogy therefore serves to highlight the difficulty of defining stages and transitions in the sublimation process, as it appears to jump and forestall such progressive assumptions. It also powerfully evokes a central formative absence - the absence of liquid fluidity - which becomes apparent when evaporation suddenly produces a fixed and solid form. There is no place for liquid symbolic elaboration, which is why the sublime emerges suddenly, and seemingly indirectly. This makes it strikingly ambivalent and ominously pleasurable - both features that characterize the Kantian sublime: 'since the mind is not simply attracted by the object, but is alternately repelled thereby, the delight in the sublime does not so much involve positive pleasure as admiration or respect i.e. it merits the name of negative pleasure' (Kant,1973, Book 2, p.91). For Kant, it is a *negative* pleasure, because the experience derives from an initial collapse of solid form - an immense stalling of the representable world - from which issues the pure transcendent 'gaseous' sublime [5]. The pleasure is negative because it '...arises only indirectly, being brought about by a momentary check to the vital forces followed at once by a discharge all the more powerful, and so it is an emotion that seems to be no sport, but dead earnest in the affairs of imagination' (Kant,1973, ibid.).

If we follow through these analogical excursions, it is easy to see why sublimation and the sublime have led psychoanalytic work in a single problematic direction: first of all, sublimation and the sublime challenge views of a 'final aim' (*Endziel*) to all instinctual drives in a 'real' world that is ordered around practical needs and desires - as the sublime is ultimately irreducible to sexual, ethical, or aesthetic criteria; secondly, the sublime is neither necessarily coextensive nor assimilable into the symbolic world - rather it marks a 'stalling', or a failure to symbolize, that feeds back into the representational world to disturb it to its symbolic roots (which is both exciting and terrifying - that is, a negative pleasure)

How can these analogical readings inform the use of sublimation and the sublime in contemporary clinical work? Laplanche suggests that the use of these terms poses a fundamental *problem of abstraction* (Laplanche, 1980, pp.29 ff.). By abstraction, he means a concrete process: 'a whole section of the theory of sublimation consists in admitting that drive energy can *abstract itself* from its sexual context. Auto-desexualization means self-induced separation from the source, object, and aim of its own drive, and the exchange of them for others' (ibid.,p.30). Although, ironically, Laplanche leaves this insight in the abstract, his indication that both the abstraction process and its product - the sublime - are *concrete*, provides a vital departure-point for the practical elaboration of the concepts in a clinical context.

How can we talk usefully of a concrete and abstract sublime in clinical sessions? Such a sublime must incorporate the following features: it must mark a sudden and unmediated shift of level of experience (analogically evoked by the solid-to-gas shift); this, in turn, must mark a shift in the mode and terms of representation (analogically evoked by desexualization and its shift from set source, object and aim towards concrete abstraction); finally, it must contain 'negative pleasure' (analogically evoked by terror and wonder at the stalling-resurge process in sublime creations).

Contemporary art is an obvious area for psychoanalysts to explore for clinical insight into the representation of the sublime. In my view, the contemporary painter most frequently associated with the representation of the sublime - Barnett Newman - provides a unique opportunity to investigate the production of the sublime in clinical experience [6]. Newman's abstractions interrupt elaborative coloured space with a single-colour vertical line he called 'the zip'. Indeed he used the term 'the zip' to mark the way he produced the line: he would stick masking tape across a canvas, elaborate the painting, and then unzip the tape. The zip therefore remained at a flatter level on the canvas, and retained the imprint of raised edges where the masking tape had protected the field. Newman associated the zip with *tsimtsum* , the primal light of creation in the *Kabbalah* (Hess, 1972, pp. 72-73), and called it the 'instant divider ..that captures the "HERE"' - that is, all that escapes the 'associative and historical' process of other colours and scenes: 'Here I am, *here* ... and out beyond there is chaos, nature, rivers, landscapes...' (Newman, 1949; cf.Lyotard, 1991, pp.78 ff.)

Newman's conception of the production-dynamics of the

zip provides a useful analogy to help us approach and understand the operation of the sublimation process in the clinical session. There are moments in analysis when the accumulation of a patient's de-translative work on scenes and narratives, provokes an instant emptying of their power. As with the rip of Newman's masking tape, this strikes a single furrow between previous scenes and stories which cannot be reintegrated into them. This zip then resurges as a magical but vital challenge, if not threat, to the place and coherence of what previously seemed to make sense.

The zip is experienced as both deeper than the adjoining scenes and stories, and also singularly emptier. As the patient looks down vertically through various connected scenes and stories, the zip literally empties out the associative and evocative power. This can provoke extreme and ambivalent emotions, such as 'seeing the light', 'touching the bottom', 'getting to the root' of crucial life experience, or 'falling out' of reality into some boundary-less expanding space. In all cases, it is the mixture of depth - of seeing right down through a symptom, across its labyrinth of connecting offshoots - with the sensation of emptying or hollowing out [7], that produces the sublime. The zip is therefore profoundly ambivalent: ultimately real and hallucinatory, terrifying and liberating, unburdening and compulsive, self-authorizing and disempowering, and life-renewing and deadening.

How then can the zip ever fit into analysis? In important ways, it leads back into primary sensory material, and away from symbolic reprocessing or construction (see above Chapter 6). As the zip-teeth of old narrative connections unlock, the empty connecting space fills with the remaining unprocessed psychic material. Almost inevitably, the zip snares up deep down there with primal ideal and identificatory scenes, so that the sublime resurge of power becomes overwhelmingly pre-genital, and visual/auditory rather than verbal. In the post-zip working-through, there is often the

introduction of newly 'found' pure and ideal love-relation-
ships, which are markedly de-sexualized, or riven by impo-
tence; and these suddenly become zipped-off from the 'lust'
for sex with long-term partners. Such zip-offs are often pre-
pared, and then enhanced, in dreams: the deeper down the
zip, the sparser the dream-landscape - rooms become emptier
- and the colour becomes more primal; in the up-zips, dreams
fill up with people and things - landscapes and rooms develop open vistas - and relationship (including transference)
becomes increasingly fraught and problematic.

*

A man of 35, an only child, has 'mourning and relationship
problems' (to quote the general practitioner's referral note).
He is a consultant cardiologist with a flourishing career. He is
a handsome man, who takes inordinate care of his appearance. He works out daily, has his hair cut regularly, and
spends large amounts of money on sunshine holidays and
new clothes. He has five children from different relationships,
but only 'takes care' of the last two, who were conceived by
his present partner. By 'takes care', he means living with, and
participating in all the family duties associated with these
children. He gives generous financial support for the others,
but rarely sees them. He has never married, but one of the
main items on his agenda when he first comes to see me is
whether to marry his present partner or not. He does not love
her, but then he has never loved any of his partners. He does,
however, love his last two children.

He has been sexually promiscuous since the age of 16 - the
age he left home. In the summer before he left, he had taken
to spying on his parents as they made love. This excited him
enormously, and developed into quite an obsession. On one
hot evening, he left the scene before his parents finished cop-
ulating, and went out into the garden to masturbate. The

young woman next door, who was a few years older than him, came out of her ground floor bedroom into the garden to see what was happening. They 'hugged and embraced, but did not "French-kiss"', and, for the first time in his life, he felt 'blissful and fully understood'.

In his frequent references to this scene, he increasingly polarises the inner and outer spaces: the parental copulation becomes classified as 'a sordid little routine' and 'unendingly boring'; and the garden encounter becomes 'totally and absolutely beautiful' and a 'once-in-a-lifetime experience'. He also becomes convinced that his parents never truly loved each other, and should have split up when they first fully realized it (which he surmised happened before his mother conceived him). In contrast, the woman next door becomes increasingly desired and enigmatic. He fantasizes about the colour of her eyes, and the shape of her body, though never in an explicitly sexual way. She remains 'simply beautiful'. He has not seen her since that last summer, and, in fact, has gone out of his way not to meet her again.

His parents died within a few months of each other six years ago. He saw them frequently in the years preceding their death, but through 'duty rather than affection'. The family's final year together had been full of conflict. He had written independently to both his parents to express his disappointment with them, and to suggest that they 'bite the bullet' and split up. They both responded hostilely to his proposal, and suggested he look rather at his own shortcomings in love relations, and his inability to find a wife. As I mentioned, his two main reasons for coming into analysis were to 'deal with the difficulties of his mourning', and to decide whether his present partner should become his wife.

In the third session, he announces that he has fallen madly in love with a young junior doctor. From first glance across a busy ward, he was totally captured by her beauty. He felt lifted out of the 'hot sordid' surroundings ('sordid' is also the word used to describe the parental copulation), and suddenly plunged into 'warmth, peace, and tranquillity'. He compares himself enthusiastically with Swann in the first volume of Proust's *A la Recherche du Temps Perdu* (his favourite novel). He strongly resists my gentle intimation that Swann's *'coup de foudre'* was a prelude to Proustian disillusionment, rather than the fullness of pleasure, and launches into a long disquisition on the vital importance of 'special moments'. He lists a number of his own special moments: on the beach in summer with the reddest of sunsets over the sea; on a bridge on an icy cold winter evening with the stars so bright in the sky; and lying in the grass in a glade in the midst of a huge forest, listening to the rustle of leaves. His summer encounter with his young beautiful neighbour is curiously absent from this list. In each of these scenes, he is alone, but certain that a nameless beloved woman is about to appear who will know exactly how he feels. In each scene, he is serene, but equally aware of ominous forces all round that will soon destroy the moment.

He takes the junior doctor to the theatre. At dinner afterwards, they discuss their mutual attraction, and return to her flat to make love. He feels 'enraptured' and deeply in love with her, but is unable to achieve erection. He tells me that this does not unduly trouble him, as this situation has happened before. He is unconcerned whether it troubles his new lover. He describes the bedroom scene in great detail, drawing attention to her locking the door and dimming the lights - which 'put him to rest'. He gives no sexual detail whatsoever, which is unusual for him. Instead, he talks of 'a strange sensation of the light getting slowly brighter behind her head' (she was on top of him), and a 'deep sonorous sigh' that slowly gets louder. He talks first of terror - terror that someone was watching and slowly turning up the dimmer switch - and then 'massive relief' and 'pure joy', which was triggered initially by the thought that the sighing might just be the air conditioning. He falls asleep 'in bliss', though is woken up by his lover, who is very alarmed and tells him he passed out. He says that she thought she had lost him, and it was so wonderful for him to realize that someone really loved him. Despite her protest, he decides to go home immediately. Once home, he goes straight to bed. When his partner complains about his lateness, he 'fucks her senseless'.

The love affair persists in this manner for several months. His accounts of their encounters remain on the threshold of delusion, and he stretches out on the couch and becomes sleepy and trance-like when describing her presence. He continues to fail to achieve erection, but dismisses her idea that he may be 'impotent' with her, because he is 'so full of bliss and desire for her'. He also continues to return home and have 'sordid' sex with his partner, whom he berates for 'being so ugly and boring'.

His dream-life burgeons (previously, he dreamt rarely and 'unspectacularly'). He reports one 'dream' in particular - which could also have been a 'half-asleep fantasy' - where he is on a beach at gloaming, and spots a naked woman afloat in the sea. Her body gently lifts with the swell of the sea. She is serenely happy - he can tell, but does not know why. In the midst of this beautiful sight, he is suddenly struck by her pubic hair, which is 'jet black, and thick, and glistens in the last rays of light'. The pubic hair grows rapidly larger 'as if it punctures a hole in the picture', and it becomes a large furry insect flying towards him. He is terrified and looks around to see hundreds of these insects in the sky. He then becomes peaceful, and sees that they are inordinately beautiful. They fly round his head and rub their fur affectionately into his face. He feels serene, and speculates (in his dream) that the naked woman must have felt the same.

This dream/half-asleep fantasy is a zip that reveals fundamental connections for him between earlier sublime moment/scenes. Within the simple figural dream/fantasy shifts, he is particularly struck by the stark inversion from looking out at a naked woman, to the pubic hair-insect rushing in on him ominously (and then lovingly) on the 'last rays of light'. He associates this with the inversion of looking in on the parental copulation, then rushing out into the other encounter with his neighbour. He also becomes sensitive to the central function and change of light in his 'sublime' moments, particularly to the polarity between absence of any sexual detail or effect (in the bedroom scene), and highlight of the other person's sexual characteristics (in the beach scene) . In association, he notes that he has no recollection either of the colour and shape of his mother's pubic hair, or of his father's pubic hair, or of his new lover's pubic hair (he speculates that she may have shaved it off); it never dawns on him (before the dream) to think whether the young woman next door has pubic hair, because she cannot be 'sordid'. In contrast, he feels he can never love his partner, precisely because he is 'ever aware' and bored by her sexual characteristics - but he nevertheless always 'fucks her senseless'.

Particular abstract features of his zip-experience persist and trouble him. He remains simultaneously worried and fascinated by the black colour and matted texture of the fur on the insect's body. He feels it is somehow 'traumatic' - a 'black hole in the picture' that threatens to 'collapse the whole world'; but it is also deeply comforting 'in a resigned sort of way' - and he associates the matted texture with his mother's sweater she had once pulled over him when he was cold.

The zip then did not intimate any analytic resolution of the paradoxes (Kantian 'negative pleasures') encapsulated in his various sublime moments. It did, however, literally cast light on the rhizome and connecting roots of his experience of romantic 'love', and its affective insulation from sexual desire and potency. At least analytic work after the zip enabled him to begin to look at this 'love' as a de-translation of parental copulation - a de-translation that snared up with important primary unprocessed sensorial material (articulated at zip-bottom by the colour black and matted texture). Such analytic work certainly did not remove his need for the sublime moment - or indeed for more zips - but simply furthered contact with specific ways in which the sublime figured in his own sublimation process. It remains a moot point whether he can ever branch out beyond his form of 'love', or be sexual with those he loves, or love those he 'fucks senseless'.

[1] Although Strachey's translation (of 'civilization' and its 'discontents') misses the specific context of Freud's German terms, Freud himself intriguingly comments in *The Future of an Illusion* that the distinction between *Kultur* and *Zivilisation* is not fundamental to him (SE.XXI,p6). Furthermore, in the first three versions of the text, culture was qualified by 'unhappiness' (das *Unglück*) rather than 'dis-ease' (das *Unbehagen*).

[2] It is important to note here that Alice Strachey, the English translator of Klein, conflates and misses the distinction in German between *Wiedergutmachung* (reparation) and *Wiederherstellung* (restitution) [cf.Stanton, 1991,p.180].

[3] *Bildung* in German (derived from *Bild*, a picture) denotes both culture and individual education.

[4] Of course, 'orthodox' Lacanians also adhere to the primacy of the Oedipus Complex - whereas post-Lacanians (notably Laplanche, Kristeva and Irigaray) regard it as secondary. This has led to a basic, and often unsophisticated, exchange in which some 'orthodox' Lacanians accuse post-Lacanians of positively promoting homosexuality, and some post-Lacanians accuse 'orthodox' Lacanians of homophobia.

[5] There are interesting parallels here with Jung's exploration of the alchemical process as a metaphor for transference (Jung, 'Psychology of the Transference [1946]', in Jung, *Collected Works.*,vol.16).

[6] Barnett Newman (1901-1970), an abstract expressionist painter from the New York school, specifically addressed the issue of the sublime in both his writings ('The Sublime is Now' [1948]) and his paintings ('Vir Heroicus Sublimis' [1950-1951]). This work has been central to the development of post-modernist critique of the notion: particularly important here is Jean-Francois Lyotard's reading of Newman's transgression of event-bound and elaborative time with a sublime 'instant' time of a single line of colour ('Newman: The Instant', in Lyotard, 1991).

[7] cf. Jean Laplanche's notion of the 'hollowed out' transference (*transfert en creux*) mentioned above, p. 52

CHAPTER 10

CONCLUSION
TACT AND THE DEVELOPMENT OF TECHNIQUE

Freud made relatively few pronouncements on psychoanalytic technique, and what he did say - notably in his celebrated 'Papers on Technique' (1911-15, S.E.XII) - is tersely pragmatic and scarcely conceptually developed. Strachey, in his 'Editor's Introduction' to the Papers, suggests that Freud 'certainly disliked the notion of future patients knowing too much about the details of his technique', adding that 'this feeling is exemplified by his proposal...to restrict the circulation of a work on technique to a limited number of analysts' (Freud, S.E. XII, p.87).

Even so, the few substantive comments that Freud does make about technique highlight the precarious and paradoxical nature of psychoanalytic work itself. He is at great pains to substantiate that this precariousness and paradox are not simply generated by the 'resistance' of the patient, but by the unique abnormality of the analytic situation itself. Unlike 'ordinary' relationships, psychoanalysis involves neither reciprocity nor affective exchange. In fact, Freud 'cannot advise [his] colleagues too urgently to model themselves during psychoanalytic treatment on the surgeon, who puts aside all his feelings, even his human sympathy, and concentrates his mental forces on the single aim of performing the operation as skilfully as possible' (Freud, S.E.XII, p.115). Freud's justification for this fundamental 'emotional coldness' is that it 'creates the most advantageous conditions for both parties: for the doctor a desirable protection for his own emotional life and for the patient the largest amount of help that we can give him today' (ibid.). To support this justification, he adds the famous motto of the French surgeon Ambroise Paré: 'Je le pansai, Dieu le guérit' ('I dressed his wounds, God cured him').

There are important implications in this surgical analogy. First of all, it is implied that the analyst makes the patient bleed, and counts on God - or the forces of nature - to heal the wounds. Secondly, it is taken to be paramount that the analyst-surgeon protects his own emotional life, and that this is achieved only by 'emotional coldness'. Thirdly, the patient is assumed to be best served by scientific objectivity, and therefore empathy or emotional support become potentially detrimental to the analytic process.

Each of these implications reinforces the notion that technique is impersonal and mechanical. An analyst, like a surgeon-doctor, needs to determine the correct diagnosis, fully understand the mechanics of psychic function, and know how to use the knife efficiently. Like all mechanics, the analyst must obey the fundamental rules - an 'obedience' Freud analogically extends into various areas of the physical world; the analyst, for example, is ordered to 'adjust himself to the patient as a telephone receiver is adjusted to the transmitting microphone' (a curious analogy, given Freud's notorious dislike of telephones! S.E.XII, pp.115-116).

It is not difficult to see how this conception of technique developed into an obsession with obeying and maintaining the 'fundamental rules', at the necessary expense of ignoring the underlying relational dynamic - notably Freud's concern to 'protect' the emotional life of the analyst, balanced by the patient's supposed belief in the beneficence of God or the forces of nature. Much current concern to secure 'rigorous standards' in analysis, for example, trades on this mechanistic reading of technique, in which the 'rules' and 'laws' to be obeyed are simply formal procedural structures such as the requisite number and time of sessions, or the diagnostic-category-status of training patients, or the appropriate status of the supervisor or the training analyst. Likewise, the supreme concern given to maintaining the analytic 'frame', which supplements these fixed time-vectors with suitable taboo-structures like the prohibition of touch, or the ban of any personal information about the analyst, his method, or his life circumstances (cf.Langs,1995).

This mechanistic formalism loads huge additional strain on top of the original 'unreal' nature of the analytical encounter. The encounter is no longer just 'frustrating' in its non-reciprocity - as Freud characterizes it (S.E.XII,p.118) - but wilfully denying and withholding in its dogmatic and unexplained imposition of preestablished no-go and no-discussion areas. The most dramatic tension here must emerge in the analyst's attempt to control affective, non-verbal levels of communication through interpretation, which, in itself, must be non-negotiable (if only to mark out the supposed 'boundaries'). This leads to peculiar distortions of analytic functions deemed closest to the affective boundary between analyst and patient.

'Holding', for example, is often limited in analysis to specific interpretations, and any other form of empathy (including the physical act of holding) is regarded as anathema. Patrick Casement, for example, records an extraordinary case of a patient (Mrs. B.), who asked him if she might be able to hold his hand. She had suffered a severe scalding in childhood, and her mother had traumatically withdrawn her hand prior to the child's anaesthesia (Casement, 1985, p.156ff.). Casement initially agrees to the possibility because he feels 'she needed me to be "in touch" with the intensity of her anxiety' (ibid., p.156), but a few days later withdraws his offer. What he offers her instead is an interpretation, which he argues (to her first and foremost) is more 'holding' than literally holding her hand. The interpretation itself is countertransferential, so pertains to Casement's speculative motivations rather than a perception of her needs. To him, the offer to hold her hand potentially intimated that he was offering to be a 'better mother' than her own, who had withdrawn her hand; he was afraid of losing his patient if he did not make this offer; and finally, if he did hold her hand, 'it would almost certainly not, as she assumed, help her to get through a re-experiencing of the original trauma' (p.158).

Not surprisingly, Mrs. B. is 'stunned' by Casement's change of mind (ibid.,p.159); but, even more surprisingly, Casement offers neither apology for the withdrawal of the offer, nor any speculation on what this withdrawal might impose on the affective level of their communication. Would she, or could she, for example, still trust him (if indeed she was supposed to trust him in the first place)? Instead, he asserts the 'holding' value of his interpretation, which is non-negotiable, despite the fact that it relates primarily to his own anxiety about the possibility of her leaving him , and to his offer of unsubstantiated promises concerning the 'curative' value of re-experiencing trauma. The only conceivable reason that he refuses to explore the consequences of his *volte-face* with the patient is that he believes in the self-evidence of the 'fundamental rules' and 'boundaries' - specifically, in this case, in the prohibition of touch. It remains inconceivable for him, therefore, that 'holding' here might mean any more than an interpretation that might indicate and reinforces these rules.

What is particularly striking about this reading of 'holding' is its rigidity. The analyst's fear of transgression (above all of the 'rules') is so omnipotent that there is no room to explore alternatives or *nuances*. Would the consequences of holding this patient's hand inevitably be so cataclysmic? The fear here is obviously of crossing a boundary and reaching a point of no return - to be 'in touch' at this point means holding on to the right to withdraw. If you hold this patient's hand, will you have to keep on holding this patient's hand in every subsequent session if she requests it? Will it provoke demands for more intimate forms of holding?

Above all, these questions impute that the patient is inevitably manipulative and seductive in her/his need to be held. This may well be the case, but it is not inevitably so. It is also possible that the request of very distressed patients to have their hand held might express a basic human need - which does not wish to smash down barriers or establish a precedent. Not to hold their hand in this context could well be read as inhuman, or sadistically denying, or simply 'out of touch'. The point here is that there are no general 'rules' that can predetermine this specific decision. In each case, it is up to the analyst to set the context for any form of holding, or with-holding[1]. If the feared manipulations and seductions do indeed occur, then the analyst is as much, if not more involved than the patient her or himself[2].

*

To stay 'in touch' with the patient requires maximum flexi-bility or 'elasticity' of technique (to use Ferenczi's noteworthy term) [Ferenczi, 'The Elasticity of Psychoanalytic Technique', 1928, in Ferenczi, 1955]. Ferenczi suggests that this require-ment can be met by the analyst's development of 'tact' - a par-ticularly appropriate term, given its specific associative span between the tactile and the cultivation of emotionally sensi-tive behaviour. These associations are further enriched by the original German term *der Takt*, which adds the musical sense of 'time', 'beat', or 'measure'. In German, a conductor's baton is a *Taktierstock*, and this opens up the additional problem of working out appropriate *tempi* in life: *dem Takt bringen lassen*, for example, means to disconcert someone, or to put them off their stroke.

Ferenczi's notion of 'tact' has been vitally transformative in the development of non-surgical models of psychoanalytic technique, and, perhaps for this very reason, subject to crass and uncritical derision. Particularly important here is Ferenczi's notion that 'tact' requires *activity* (the 'active tech-nique'): a particular *mutual form of activity* in which the ana-lyst's (active) tact potentially nourishes useful and attainable areas of activity within the patient. The skill here - and Ferenczi was very absorbed with this *artisan* nature of psychotherapy - is to develop some sense of what the patient can register, and what kind of potential for critical disentanglement may be explored in the context of the present session and/or as a future prospect: 'I have come to the conclusion that it is above all a question of psychological tact whether or when one should tell the patient some particular thing, when the material [s]he has produced should be considered sufficient to draw conclusions, in what form these should be presented to the patient, how one should react to an unexpected or bewildering reaction on the patient's part, when one should keep silent and await further associations, and at what point the further maintenance of silence would result only in causing the patient useless suffering' (Ferenczi, 'The Elasticity of Psychoanalytic Technique'[1928], 1955, p.89).

To develop tact, the analyst has to place her or himself in a certain position, and determining that position requires 'elasticity' - which is where the skill comes in. By 'elasticity', Ferenczi means flexibility in response to the patient's emotional output. Analysts must learn to negotiate skilfully both the patient's and their own ambivalences, without lapsing into cold assertion of their own power or authority: he warns that 'nothing is more harmful for the analysis than a schoolmasterish, or even an authoritative, attitude on the physician's part. Anything we say to the patient should be put to him in the form of a tentative suggestion and not of a confidently held opinion, not only to avoid irritating him[/her], but because there is always the possibility that we may be mistaken.' (Ferenczi, 1955, p.94). Similarly, analysts should remain sympathetic (or 'elastic') when confronted with both effusive empathy - such as total 'faith' in the curative power of analysis - and excessive antipathy: '"antipathetic" features are in most cases only fore-structures, behind which quite different characteristics are concealed; dropping the patient in such cases would be merely leaving him in the lurch, because the unconscious aim of intolerable behaviour is often to be sent away.' (Ferenczi, 1955, p.95)

The standard criticism of Ferenczi's notion of 'elasticity' is that it exclusively develops a positive transference towards the analyst, and consequently forecloses any possibility of negative transference[3] . Although it is certainly true that Ferenczi does seek to remove offence or irritation with him because he believes it prolongs resistance, it would be wrong to view this as the full extent of his conception of 'activity'. It is important to appreciate here that 'active <$itechnique>' primarily addresses the patient's activity, notably the patient's potential for action. Ferenczi stresses in his later work that the main aim of tact is to appraise the patient's 'concealed tendencies to action' (Ferenczi, 1955, p.96). In this sense, Ferenczi's exhortation of trust and honesty in the analyst is aimed at developing a certain mutual recognition of the limitations of any supposed 'cure'. In the end, he is advocating that analytic technique should aim to promote some kind of mutual constructive realism, similar in many ways to that proposed by Winnicott. In this context, he would certainly corroborate Winnicott's conviction (reported by Masud Khan) that '...the most important lesson is that one must not try to cure a patient beyond his need and his psychic resources to sustain and live from that cure' (Winnicott, 1986, p.18)

*

However flawed or restricted in its elaboration[4], Ferenczi's notion of tact opens up radical options in psychoanalytic technique . Above all, it highlights the problematics of *position* and *direction* in analysis. Ferenczi suggests that it is possible for the analyst to *take a position*, and, of course, to be 'flexible' with it, and modify it; and it is possible as well, within this tactful activity, to *direct the course of analysis* simply by taking up a position. By this, he emphasizes that the analyst can actively prepare the end of the analysis, or shorten it - so that the appropriate technical question then becomes one of actively *terminating* analysis, rather than assuming that a termination simply comes about and is mutually recognized by the analyst and patient (Ferenczi,'The Problem of the Termination of Analysis' [1927], 1955).

With consummate tact, Ferenczi reminds us that the problem of taking a position in the analytical session is first of all a practical one. Where do patients position themselves? Do they sit on a chair? If so, how is the chair positioned? Does the analyst let the patient choose or modify the position of the chair? Or does the analyst insist that the patient lie on the couch? In answer to these questions, Ferenczi proposes yet again a tactful flexibility. Certain anxious or more psychotic patients need to maintain eye-contact, and need to stay 'in touch' with the analyst's visible responses. Other more narcissistic and neurotic patients form an immediate *penchant* for the non-visually-communicative space of the couch. Others still need to explore and occupy the different spaces on offer. Sometimes they will need to sit up and face the analyst, or move around the room.

The crucial question surrounding such flexibility is the exercise of power and authority. To what extent does the analyst prescribe or proscribe the analytic situation by the material setting - the positioning of chairs, the couch, and the initial description of how the analytic process is supposed to proceed[5]? To answer this question - with specific reference to Ferenczi - Lacan suggests analogically extending the problematic of positioning into the area of games - card-games in particular, and specifically bridge (Lacan, 'The Direction of the Treatment and The Principles of Its Power', in Lacan, 1977, pp.246-247). In this analogy, Lacan proposes that the analyst occupies the position of the 'dummy' in bridge - that is, of the partner of the 'declarer', the player who plays to win.

The 'dummy' has an added significance in French - as the term *le mort* (the dummy) also connotes the corpse: the phrase *'faire le mort'* means to play dead, or to lie low. In bridge, Lacan reminds us, the dummy is there both to indicate who is leading (that is, the declarer/patient), and to develop a strategy of trying to expose the hand of the fourth player. At this point - as Nick Totton has recently cogently illustrated - Lacan's analogy invites endless metapsychological speculation about who might constitute the fourth player: is it possible, for example, that the dummy might be the partner of the fourth player, in which case the patient becomes the dummy; alternatively, analysts might *choose* to play before or after the fourth player, and thus determine to position themselves as the dummy? (Totton, 1996). Totton sensibly opts for the latter option - which stresses that the analyst must *intervene* as the dummy, by 'cadaverizing his position' as Lacan put it (Lacan, 1977, p.140): 'the analyst, in good classic form, lies low, avoiding a response to the transference, allowing themselves to be pulled and propped passively in place, while at the same time remorselessly "acting on the resistances that weigh down, impede and divert speech"...' (Totton, 1996, pp.33-34).

However awkward and formalistic the bridge analogy, it does relate the analyst's position to a powerful equation of non-responsiveness and death: it proposes that the analyst's intervention necessarily evolves around 'playing dead'. To what purpose? Following Lacan, the active assumption of the 'dead' position must aim to reveal the transference in all its 'otherness' (its unprocessability or untranslatability) - that is, to force the hand of the fourth player, the significant 'other' (the protagonist) [see above Chapter 5, p48] that counters and obstructs the patient's 'lead'; counters and obstructions that in turn *emboss* the transference (Laplanche's *le transfert en plein*). 'To play dead' in this analogy means not to play to win, but to play to reveal the other's hand. The other thing (*Das Andere*) - as opposed to the other person (*Der Anderer*) - in this game is death, which, in this analogy, is all that lies outside the subject and perception. To take account of death in the play of analysis therefore implies a sense of *what is shut off* from (and, to some extent, by) the subject in the psychic process itself. The process through which the analyst reveals the fourth player's hand - namely all that is shut off from the subject - bears a striking resemblance to the strategy Ferenczi termed 'the wisdom of clairvoyance'[6]: 'a paraphrase of the old adage: the wiser one gives in. Or more correctly: he (she) who gives in becomes wiser. Or better still: the person struck by a trauma comes into contact with death i.e. with the state in which egotistic tendencies and defensive measures are shut off, above all resistance by friction, which in the egotistic form of existence brings about the isolation of objects and the self in time and space. In the moment of the trauma some sort of omniscience about the world associated with a correct estimation of the proportions of the own and foreign powers and a shutting out of any falsification by emotivity (i.e. pure objectivity, pure intelligence) makes the person in question - even after consequent consolidation - more or less clairvoyant.' (Ferenczi 'Notes and Fragments, 2.4.1931', in Ferenczi, 1955, p.243)

Aside from the familiar heroic overestimation of the analyst's 'power' visible again here - notably in the assumption of 'omniscience', 'correct estimation', 'pure objectivity', 'pure intelligence', and so forth - Ferenczi remarkably locates the two main technical issues posed by the analyst's position first in trauma, and the confrontation with otherness (the '(con)*tact* with death'); and second, in the resultant issue of the 'proportions of the own and foreign powers', which is actively provoked by 'the falsification by emotivity'. In this formulation, 'trauma' is originally formed around the direct confrontation with the other and otherness (death or non-ego); and the 'proportional' problem subsequently forms around the isolation of 'objects' and 'self' in time and space[7].

*

The main practical contention emerging from these various analogical speculations is that it is possible for analysts to determine a position for themselves in each analysis which will mark out in optimum relief the contours of unconscious unprocessed material which the patient inevitably brings to relationships. This position may vary within each analysis, and between different analyses, but there is nonetheless a common technique based on the establishment of trust, openness, and flexibility. The analyst has to shift as necessary, and secure flexibility - if necessary, by admitting mistakes, apologizing, acknowledging significant gestures, gifts, greeting cards, and so forth - in order to remain 'in touch'. There is no difference here between the analytical relationship and any other caring and mutually respectful relationship. The difference lies in the capacity to shift within these parameters specifically to highlight the opaque painful areas of relationship - or the *contundors* (see Chapter 7 p79); and this capacity constitutes a skill in the broadest sense of the word[8].

The issue then is whether such a skill is transmittable or teachable, or whether it is uniquely personal and empathic (as some would argue is the case with 'clairvoyance'). The analyst's skill in the session revolves around discerning how and where to move in order to enable the patient to see what neither fits nor works in their own feelings and perceptions in analysis. The analyst's decision to shift must itself be articulated within the analysis - even within the act of remaining silent, of apologizing, or deciding to hold the patient's hand to stay 'in touch'. Indeed, analysts have their positions marked, and must mark their shift of position, whether it follows set 'rules' (or their sense of determination within them) or not.

I suggest that an appropriate term for this skill is *alignment*[9]: analysts must endeavour to align themselves with the fourth player (in the bridge analogy), that is, they must position themselves in direct relation to the contundors, the sensitive areas of unprocessed material. In the first instance, this term must be taken literally, and the analyst must explore and become familiar with shared visual ground within the session - that is where the analyst and patient's gaze can meet and mutually interrelate (see figs. 1 & 2); as well as exploring the non-seen, where the analyst and patient respectively either uniquely receive sounds (the voice of the other) or speculate and fantasize (for example, has the analyst fallen asleep?!) The analyst needs above all to adopt alignment with the non-seen space: to be 'in touch', for example, if the patient does speculate that (s)he has fallen asleep (presuming, of course, that they have not!), so that the form, sense and direction of the patient's paranoid intrusion can be addressed.

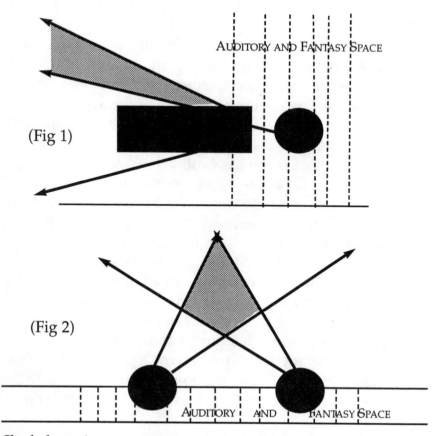

Shaded area is common gaze, arrows indicate perceptual vectors

Secondly, alignment issues emerge preeminently in trans-ference-stallings, particularly when the patient becomes convinced that the analyst is wilfully insensitive, or when the analyst becomes convinced that the patient is not addressing them but someone else. In such cases, alignment for the analyst involves identifying that 'other' position, and, if necessary, directly addressing it. This does not mean, for example, directly relating to a patient that it is 'really' their father who they fear has gone to sleep, because their father was never there, or never paid attention. Rather, to become 'in touch' with the complex and diffuse form of those contundors that the patient temporarily locates behind their head: the contundors, for example, could articulate complex links between anxiety surrounding specific loss or absence; this anxiety - or anger (at the sleepful state) - could be *projective*, perhaps at the prospect of the end of the session, or at the recalled sight of the analyst as 'tired' or 'pale'. Another potential here is that, in the transference-stalling, the contundor has emerged in reaction to unprocessed material in the analyst, and that the analyst's sense of provocation feeds back into the development of the session. In all cases here, alignment for the analyst indicates staying in touch with the contundor, and not attempting to dismiss or foreclose it through a construction.

*

To end with a clinical example: an apt one, in that it concerns 'ending' before a holiday break. A married man, with no children, in his mid-40s, is referred to me on account of marital problems. He complains that his wife is too domineering. She shouts until she gets her way. His attempts to counter her have usually provoked extreme mutual distress, in which she falls 'ill' - she has had a spinal complaint since childhood and any conflict brings on intense back pain - and he feels suicidally depressed. He has attempted suicide once, four years ago, but took too few pills. A recurrent theme in the early sessions is whether he 'unconsciously knew' that he had taken too few pills to kill himself. He is surprised, but 'strangely grateful' that his wife discovered him and rushed him to hospital. He felt sure she would have liked him dead - but this idea makes him feel even more guilty. He suffers from chronic premature ejaculation, and describes himself as 'supremely unconfident' with women. He says he could only bring himself to see a male therapist.

Two months into the three-times-a-week analysis, we face the Easter Break. A month before the Break, he starts the session by announcing that he had 'better get on with things' as Easter will soon be with us, and he lies on the couch for the first time. He immediately gets up again, and sits in the chair he usually occupies, though turns it obliquely away from me, so that he does not have to look me directly in the eyes.

There is a long silence in which he blinks rapidly and emphatically, and then closes his eyes. Precisely a week later, he goes back to the couch and lies on it without hesitation. Precisely a week after that, he misses a session without warning, and attends the next 25 minutes late. He keeps his coat on, walks away from me to look out of the window, and announces that he cannot go on with the analysis, as he feels that I am 'giving him nothing'. When I ask him why he missed the previous session without warning me, he denies that we had arranged it - even though it was a regular session. He tells me anyway that the whole issue is irrelevant, because we will soon have to end for Easter, and he will feel much better - 'in control' - if he ends it first. I say that I understand his feelings. He asks me if I am angry with him, and I tell him that I am not (which is true at that time!). He walks round the room, stares at the few books I have on a shelf, takes off his coat and arranges it very neatly on the chair, walks to the couch, puffs up and reorganizes the cushions, and lies down on it. He places one cushion under his head.

He begins to talk at length about his mother. He tells me that his mother is a hard and bitter woman. She married a man much older than her, who had died of a heart-attack when their four sons were very young. She had to bring up the family on her own, which she found very hard, despite the fact that money was no object, and *au-pairs* and servants were always on hand. He tells me that he can remember very little about either his mother or his father in his childhood. His father was always away at work, and often travelled abroad. He remembers his mother coming in to the nursery one day and announcing in a matter-of-fact way that their father had had a heart-attack and died. A firm was called in to 'sort out' his father's things. My patient is convinced that his mother is the most indifferent to him because he is the eldest. When I ask him why he thinks this, he speculates that it has some-thing to do with her relationship to his father: his father 'pulled the wool over her eyes' (the mother's expression), and, as the first-born son, he had to bear all the resentment later. He tells me with great emotion (a mix of excitement and anger) that he is certain that his father had 'lots' of affairs, but he has, and had, no way of substantiating this, as his father (and father's family) remain so distant.

In the course of these sessions, I come into 'touch' with the particular sensitivity he bears towards distance. He wants me to keep a certain distance - but not too close (or he turns away his chair), or too far: if I had 'interpreted' his missed session, he would have felt deeply rejected, and perhaps 'ended' everything there. On the other hand, the impending question of 'ending' the sessions for Easter both impels him to get clos-er before it is too late - that is, to lie on the couch - and to cut things off abruptly in order to 'take control'. By staying in 'touch' with these powerful ambivalences, and not interven-ing interpretatively, he was able to rehearse leaving (by miss-ing a session), and to associate his feelings of distance with his mother, and, through her, with his father. In my terms, I was not responding to his actions towards me - such as missing the session, arriving late, and so forth - but aligning with the contundors, the unprocessed ambivalence to first the mother and then the father.

It was crucial in this process also to allow him to realign his position within the sessions by an 'elastic' rather than cold rule-orientated response (which would have further stalled the analysis by despair at the mother and anger/fear of loss towards the father). Similarly, his move to the couch was enabled by my absence of response, rather than formal insistence on the so-called analytical frame and boundaries.

Crucial, in this respect, were the cushions, which he lovingly puffed out, and realigned prior to lying down. In the last session before the Easter Break, he asked me whether he might 'look after' one until 'next time'. I instantly agreed. In the first session after the Break, he did not realign the other cushions as he had done previously, but simply put the cushion he had 'looked after' under his head. Crucial associated scenes then emerged. He recalled first how his mother had moved him from his bedroom one year to be able to accommodate a new second *au-pair*, and had relocated him in the box room. The box room progressively filled up with junk, which made him feel even more that he had no space of his own, and indeed that there was no room for him at all. Finally, he recalled a traumatic incident at the age of about four in which his mother had given away his teddy to charity, suggesting that a boy of his age was too old to be seen with such a thing. He was heartbroken, but never managed to muster the courage to ask for it back, or to express his anger and outrage. By tactfully providing him with the space to align the cushion with the lost teddy, he was able to come back after the Break and explore lighter rooms with less junk.

[1] The prodigious subtlety of Winnicott's definition of 'holding' stands in contrast to later uses: for him, the analyst's holding 'often takes the form of conveying in words at the appropriate moment something that shows that the analyst knows and understands the deepest

anxiety that is being experienced. Occasionally holding must take a physical form, but I think this is only because there is a delay in the analyst's understanding which he can use for verbalizing what is afoot. There are times when you carry round your child who has earache. Soothing words are no use. Probably there are times when a psychotic patient needs physical holding, but eventually it will be understanding and empathy that will be necessary' (Winnicott, 1965, p.240).

2 For a provocative study of the 'sadistic' input of the analyst in the 'doctor-mode', see Ernst Simmel, 'The "Doctor Game", Illness, and the Profession of Medicine', in Fliess (1948):
'...he may indulge his aggressive, sadistic tendencies in a special way in the role of operator ("the love of the knife"), in order by giving active expression to castration-*pleasure* to spare himself castration-*anxiety*' (p.262).

3 This was Melanie Klein's criticism of her own analyst: 'Technique at this time was extremely different from what it is at present (1953) and the analysis of the negative transference did not enter. I had a very strong positive transference and I feel that one should not understate the effect of that, though, as we know, it can never do the whole job' (Klein, 1953, p.42)

4 The most obvious difficulties arise around the assumption of critical and empathic accuracy on behalf of the analyst. Such assumptions, however, are not unique to Ferenczi. Bion's assumption, for example, that analysts can make efficient and effective interpretative distinctions between various levels of mental process (alpha and <$ibeta elements>, conceptual etc.), and process them in a 'grid', presupposes all sorts of 'mental gymnastics' within the session itself (Bion, 1988, pp.59-61). A converse position starts with the assumption that there are residual and accumulative areas of misrecognition in both analyst and patient, and that these themselves are subject to primary, non-translatable unconscious structures of the communicative interaction itself (notably transference).

5 The psychoanalytic session is certainly a 'spectacle' - to follow Guy Debord's felicitous expression (Debord,1983) - staged (more or less consciously) to accommodate the expectations of consumer in line with the 'demand assessment' of the provider. Hence the required couch, armchairs, white-noise-machine, ethnic rug, artwork etc., independent of any use-value. Unfortunately (so far as I know) no one has yet subjected consulting rooms to stringent situationist critique.

6 Ferenczi's use of the term 'clairvoyance' is often misunderstood, and subjected to ridicule. It is interesting, in this context, that he maintained that animals were more 'clairvoyant' than humans because their perception was not obscured by thought-projection, identification and transference.

7 Here again Ferenczi's work appears to prefigure Laplanche - particularly Laplanche's views on the 'essentially traumatic nature of human sexuality' (Laplanche, 'Why the Death Drive?', in Laplanche, 1976, p.105).

8 A 'skill' in Old English indicated the power of discrimination, particularly of what is 'powerful, proper, right or just'.

9 I have chosen this term 'alignment' fully mindful of its association with ancient burial sites. These sites clearly and literally reflected the need to bring into direct correspondence the psychic and the material worlds, and the upperworlds and underworlds. The alignments therefore literally put death in its place - and enabled the living to establish directions and 'rights' towards it. The Breton poet Guillevic poignantly writes of the alignments in his native town Carnac: 'De la mer aux menhirs, des menhirs à la mer, la même route avec deux vents contraires, et celui de la mer plein du meurtre de l'autre......Alignés, les menhirs, comme si d'être en ligne, devait donner des droits' (From the sea to the menhirs, from the menhirs to the sea, the same road with two opposite winds, and the one from the sea is full of the murder of the other...Aligned, the menhirs, as if being in line ought to give them some rights) [Guillevic, 'Carnac' p.150 & p.196, in Guillevic, 1963]

BIBLIOGRAPHY

Abraham, N. & Torok, M. (1986), *The Wolf Man's Magic Word*, Minneapolis: University of Minnesota Press.

Aron,L. & Harris, A. eds. (1993), *Sándor Ferenczi's Legacy*, New York:Analytic Press.

Ashley, D.J. (1972), *An Introduction to the General Pathology of Tumors*, Bristol:Wright.

BCP (1997), *Register of Psychotherapists*, London:Free Associations.

Benjamin A. ed.(1993),*The Lyotard Reader*, Oxford and Cambridge: Blackwell.

Bion, W.R. (1961), *Experiences in Groups*, London:Routledge.

Bion, W.R. (1962), *Learning From Experience*, London:Karnac.

Bion, W.R. (1967), *Second Thoughts*, London:Karnac.

Bion, W.R. (1988), *Attention and Interpretation*, London:Karnac.

Boothby, R. (1991), *Death and Desire*, London:Routledge.

Bowie, M., (1991), *Lacan*, London:Fontana

Campbell, A. (1995), 'Hysteria and Litigation: coping with the real of trauma', *The Letter*, Dublin, Spring 1995.

Casement, P. (1985), *On Learning From the Patient*, London: Tavistock.

Chasseguet-Smirgel, J. (1985), *The Ego Ideal*, London:Free Association Books.

Chipkevitch, E. & Fernandes, A. (1993), 'Hypothalamic tumor associated with atypical forms of
and diencephalic syndrome', *Arquivos de Neuro-Psiquiatria*, 1993, June, vol. 51 (2), pp. 270-274.

Crowther, P. (1989), *The Kantian Sublime: From Morality to Art*, Oxford:Clarendon Press.

Debord, G. (1986), *The Society of the Spectacle*, Detroit:Black and Red.

Derrida, J. (1987), *The Post Card*, Chicago:The University of Chicago Press

DSM3R (1987), *Diagnostic and Statistical Manual of Mental Disorders. Third Edition Revised*. Washington:American Psychiatric Association.

DSM4 (1994), *Diagnostic and Statistical Manual of Mental Disorders. Fourth Edition*. Washington:American Psychiatric Association.

Dunn, R. (1996), 'Syncretic Thought and the Composition of Music', in *Teaching Transference*, ed.Stanton & Reason,London: Rebus Press.

Ehlers, H. & Crick, J., eds. (1994), *The Trauma of the Past - Remembering and Working Through*, London:Goethe Institut.

Eickhoff, F.W. (1989), 'On the "borrowed unconscious sense of guilt" and the palimpsestic structure of a symptom', *International Review of Psycho-Analysis*, 16, pp.323-329.

Eth, S. & Pynoos, R.S. eds. (1985), *Post-Traumatic Stress Disorder in Children*, Washington:American Psychiatric Association.

Fenichel, O. (1946), *The Psychoanalytic Theory of Neurosis*, London:Routledge.

Ferenczi S. (1952), *First Contributions to the Theory and Technique of Psychoanalysis*, London:Maresfield.

Ferenczi, S. (1926), *Further Contributions to the Theory and Technique of Psychoanalysis*, London:Maresfield.

Ferenczi, S. (1955), *Final Contributions to the Problems and Methods of Psychoanalysis*, London:Maresfield.

Fletcher, J. & Stanton, M. eds. (1992), *Jean Laplanche: Seduction, Translation and the Drives*, London:ICA.

Fliess, Robert [ed.] (1948), *The Psychoanalytic Reader*, New York:International Universities Press.

Forrester, J., (1990), *The Seductions of Psychoanalysis*, Cambridge: Cambridge University Press.

Foucault, M. (1973), *The Birth of the Clinic: an archeology of medical perception*, London:Routledge.

French, E. (1996), *Hope in Analysis*, PhD thesis, University of Kent, Canterbury, UK.

Freud, A (1946), *The Ego and the Mechanisms of Defence*, New York:International Universities Press.

Freud, S. (1900), *The Interpretation of Dreams*, S.E.IV and V London:Hogarth.

Freud, S. (1905), *Three Essays on the Theory of Sexuality*, S.E.VII London: Hogarth.

Freud, S. (1910), *Leonardo Da Vinci and a Memory of his Childhood*, S.E.XI London:Hogarth.

Freud, S. (1912), *Recommendations to Physicians Practising Psycho-Analysis* , S.E. XII London:Hogarth.

Freud, S. (1914), *On the History of the Psycho-analytic Movement*, S.E.XIV London:Hogarth

Freud, S. (1920), *Beyond The Pleasure Principle*, S.E.XVIII London:Hogarth.

Freud, S. (1927),*The Future of an Illusion*, S.E.XXI London:Hogarth.

Freud, S. (1933), *Why War?* S.E. XXII London:Hogarth.

Freud, S. (1937), *Constructions in Analysis*, S.E.XXIII London:Hogarth.

Freud, S. (1972),*Die Traumdeutung*, Studienausgabe Band 2, Frankfurt:Fischer.

Freud, S. & Ferenczi S. (1993), *The Correspondence of Sigmund Freud and Sandor Ferenczi*, Vol.1, Cambridge, Mass:Harvard.

Fuller, P. (1988), *Theoria: Art and the Absence of Grace*, London:Chatto and Windus.

Grosz, E. (1990), *Jacques Lacan:A Feminist Introduction*, London:Routledge.

Guillevic , E. (1963), *Sphere* , Paris:Gallimard.

Hartmann, H. (1958), *Ego Psychology and the Problem of   Adaptation*, New York: International Universities Press.

Heidegger, M. (1967), *Being and Time*, tr. J. Macquarrie & E. Robinson, Oxford:Blackwell.

Herman, J.L.(1992), *Trauma and Recovery*, New York:Basic Books.

Hess, T. (1972), *Barnett Newman*, London:Tate Gallery Publications.

Hillman, J. (1967), *Insearch: Psychology and Religion*, London:Hodder & Stoughton.

Hillman, J. (1975), *Re-Visioning Psychology*, New York:Harper & Row.

Horney, K. (1946), *Are You Considering Psychoanalysis?*, New York:Norton.

Hinshelwood, R. (1985), 'Questions of Training', London:Free Associations, 2.

Jung, C.G. (1905), 'The Reaction-Time Ratio in the Association Experiment', in Jung, *Collected Works*, vol 2 (1973), pp 221-271.London:Routledge.

Jung, C.G. (1973), *Collected Works*, Vol 4 London:Routledge.

Jung, C.G. (1973), 'Psychology of the Transference [1946]', in Jung, *Collected Works*, Vol 16 London:Routledge.

Jung, C.G., (1961),   *Freud and Psychoanalysis. Collected Works 4.*, London:Routledge.

Kant, I. (1973), *Critique of Judgement*, Oxford:Oxford University Press.

Kestenberg, J.S. (1993), 'What a psychoanalyst has learned from the Holocaust and genocide', *International Journal of Psycho-Analysis* , 774, pp. 1117-1129

Khan, M. (1963), 'The concept of cumulative trauma', *Psychoanalytic Study of the Child* , Vol. 18, pp.54-88.

Klein, M. (1953), *Autobiography* , manuscript in the Klein Trust Archive, London:Wellcome Library.

Klein, M.(1961), *Narrative of a Child Analysis* London:Hogarth

Klein, M. (1975), *Envy and Gratitude and other works 1946-1963*, London:Hogarth.

Kulka, R. et al. [ed](1990), *Trauma and the Vietnam War Generation*, New York:Brunner/Maazel.

Lacan, J. (1966), *Ecrits*, Paris:Seuil.

Lacan, J., (1972), *Seminar XXIII 'Le Sinthome'* , unpublished.

Lacan, J. (1977), *Ecrits - a selection*, London:Routledge translated by Sheridan A.

Lacan, J. (1977), *The Four Fundamental Concepts of Psychoanalysis* London:Penguin Harmondsworth.

Lacan, J. (1988), *The Seminar of Jacques Lacan Book I Freud's Papers on Technique 1953-1954*, translated by Forrester, J. Cambridge:Cambridge University Press.

Lacan, J. (1991[a]), *Seminar VIII: Le transfert*, Paris:Seuil.

Lacan, J.(1991[b]), *Le Séminaire XVII L'Envers de la Psychanalyse*, Paris:Seuil

Lacan, J. (1994), *Le Séminaire Livre 4: La Relation d'objet*, Paris:Seuil.

Lagache, D., (1993), *The Work of Daniel Lagache - Selected Writings*, London:Karnac.

Langs, R., (1995), *Clinical Practice and the Architecture of the Mind*, London:Karnac.

Laplanche, J.(1976), *Life and Death in Psychoanalysis*, Baltimore:.John Hopkins.

Laplanche, J.(1980[a]), *Problematiques 3: La Sublimation* Paris:Presses Universitaires de France.

Laplanche, J. (1980[b]), *Problematiques 4: L'inconscient et le ça*, Paris:Presses Universitaires de France.

Laplanche, J. (1989[a]), *New Foundations for Psychoanalysis*, Oxford: Blackwell.

Laplanche, J. (1989[b]), 'Terminologie Raisonnée' in *Traduire Freud*, Paris:Presses Universitaires de France.

Laplanche, J. (1993[a]), *La révolution copernicienne inachevée*, Paris:Aubier.

Laplanche, J. (1993[b]), *Le fourvoiement biologisant de la sexualité chez Freud*, Les Empêcheurs de Penser en Rond, France:Plessis-Robinson .

Laplanche, J. & Pontalis, J.-B. (1973), *The Language of Psychoanalysis*, London:Karnac.

Lowy, S. (1963), *Should You Be Psychoanalyzed?*, 2nd edition, New York: Philosophical Library.

Luel, S.A. & Marcus, P. Eds. (1984), *Psychoanalytic Reflections on the Holocaust* , New York:Ktav.

Lyotard, J.-F. (1991), *The Inhuman*, London:Polity.

Masson, J. (1989), *Against Therapy*, London:Collins.

Mitchell, J. and Rose J.(Eds.) *Feminine Sexuality*, (1982), London:McMillan.

Newman, B. (1949), *Prologue for a New Aesthetic*, New York: Harper.

Noble, D. (1995), 'Physical Injury and Psychological Trauma in Children: a clinical report', *IFPE 1994 Conference Proceedings*, March 1995.

Nunberg, H. (1955), *Principles of Psychoanalysis*, New York:International Universities Press.

Peyru, G. (1992), 'The Couch and the Immobilization of the Patient', recorded lecture, Centre for Psychoanalytic Studies, University of Kent.

Pitman, R. K. et. al (1990), 'Naloxone-Reversible Analgesic Response to Combat-Related Stimuli in PTSD: a pilot study, *Archives of General Psychiatry*, 47 (1990), pp.541-547.

Roudinesco, E.(1982), *La Bataille de Cent Ans, vol. 1*, Paris:Ramsey.

Roudinesco, E. (1993), *Jacques Lacan: esquisse d'une vie, histoire d'un système de pensée*, Paris:Fayard.

Searles, H. (1992), 'Harold Searles talks to Martin Stanton' *Free Associations*, pt.3, Vol.3, No. 27.

Schneiderman, S. (1993), *How Lacan's Ideas are used in Clinical Practice*, New Jersey:Aronson

Stanton, M.(1990), *Sandor Ferenczi: reconsidering active intervention*, New Jersey:Aronson.

Stanton, M.(1993[a]), 'Psychic Contusion: remarks on Ferenczi and trauma', *British Journal of Psychotherapy*, Summer 1993.

Stanton, M.(1993[b]), 'Painting the Nightmare: Jackson Pollock's Psychoanalytic Drawings', *Modern Painters*, Winter 1993, vol.6, number 4.

Stanton, M. (1994[a]), 'Trauma and abstraction in the squiggle game', Recorded Lecture, Winnicott Studies Day, University of Kent (to be published).

Stanton, M.(1994b), 'L'après-coup et les problèmes de figuration à l'origine du symptôme', in *Nouveaux fondements pour la psychanalyse*, Paris:Presses Universitaires de France.

Stanton, Martin (1994[c]), 'Jung's Forgotten Trauma Theory', paper given at the Society of Analytical Psychology, 13 January 1994 (to be published).

Stanton, M. (1995[a]), 'Psychic Contusion', *The Letter*, Summer 1995,number 4.

Stanton, M. (1995[b]), 'The False Dichotomy Between Applied & Clinical Psychoanalysis', in Confronting the Challenges to Psychoanalysis, ed. S Friedlander, New York:APA.

Stanton, M. and Reason D., (1996), Teaching Transference London:Rebus Press.

Thomä, H., & Cheshire, N. (1991), 'Freud's *Nachträglichkeit* and Strachey's 'Deferred Action': Trauma, Constructions and the Direction of Causality', *International Review of Psychoanalysis*, vol. 18, part 3, 1991, pp. 407-427.

Totton, N. (1996), 'Playing Our Cards Right: The Position of the Analyst', *Universities Association for Psychoanalytic Studies Newsletter*, no. 5, Winter 1996, pp. 29-37.

UKCP (1997), *National Register of Psychotherapists*, London: Routledge .

University of Tel Aviv Research Project, Progress Reports Available on CD.ROM. through *Psych. Lit.*.

Van der Kolk, B.A. (1988), 'The Trauma Spectrum: The Interaction of Biological and Social Events in the Genesis of Trauma Response', *Journal of Traumatic Stress*, 1 (1988), pp.273-290.

Wangh, M. (1968), 'A Psycho-genetic factor in the recurrence of war: symposium on psychic traumatization through social catastrophe', *International Journal of Psycho-Analysis*, 49, pp. 319-323.

Winnicott, D.W. (1965), *The Maturational Processes and the Facilitating Environment* , London:Hogarth Press.

Winnicott, D.W. (1971), *Playing and Reality*, London: Harmondsworth, Penguin.
Winnicott, D. W. (1971), *Therapeutic Consultations in Child Psychiatry* , London:Hogarth.
Winnicott, D.W. (1986), *Holding and Interpretation*, London:Hogarth.